Free Agent l

Men's Guide to Peace, Quiet and Freedom

COACH GREG ADAMS

ISBN: 978-1-7330396-1-1

DEDICATION

This is dedicated to everyone who was down from day 1. You know who you are and who you are not.

CONTENTS

ACKNOWLEDGMENTS

Thank you to everyone who supports me speaking my truth

INTRODUCTION

YOUR CONTRACT IS ABOUT TO EXPIRE

If you could look into my eyes and see what I'm thinking, you'd discover that I have the focus of a determined man and that above all else, I seek to live my life very intentionally. Over the years, I have taken steps to plan my life out as much as possible, side stepping potential pitfalls and traps that many people willingly walk right into. I'm always aware that a serious misjudgment or error could turn my life upside-down and open up a can of whoop ass, to teach me that every choice that I make has serious consequences. Of course, every human is aware of this, but too many are willing to throw caution to the wind and take unnecessary risks that they could've avoided with a little deliberation.

But, I made a HUGE mistake. It was a simple snare that befell many men before me and hopefully, with the book, only a few after me. With this book, I seek to arm men with knowledge and options that are not afforded to them unless they seek it out. This information could save a man's life.

A lot of my brothers in manhood spend thousands of dollars on books, videos and seminars that might improve their chances with women. From approaching them, to sleeping with them, or improving their marriages. They are sold, that somehow, manufactured confidence and a few lead in lines might get more women in their beds. Or, somehow, holding a masculine frame will be the key to getting women to recognize them as an alpha male. My approach is quite different. This approach could even get you more attention from women - or less. Either way, you win. You win because what you are going to create is not manufactured or hollow, it will be real and deep, and you will win with them no matter what.

I'm excited that you chose to read this story and to see what the Free Agent Lifestyle is all about. I don't intend to make this a long read, because I think books can go on too much and not get to the point fast enough. It's my purpose to make this a quick read and get you on to living your Free Agent Lifestyle.

The first part of the book is going to discuss why I chose to be a *Free Agent*. It will be the darkest part of the book, but for some, it will be an enlightenment. I often speak bluntly about these things, but like many men I've coached who have similar experiences; these issues will be a rude awakening. Most men don't discover these things until it's too late.

The next part of the book will be about the *Free Agent Lifestyle*. This is where most men will experience an awakening. Things will become bright and your life will seem limitless. I still remember the day that I chose to move from my marital home prior to my divorce. The day that I left will be etched in my mind as one of the most beautiful moments I could remember. I'd never seen the sky so blue; the grass had never been greener. The sun had never been brighter. At least, that was the effect it had on me. I'd reached a level of freedom that many men are too scared to realize. If that's you, I want you to experience this freedom if you find yourself boxed in.

By the end of this book, you will be ready to make better decisions regarding your life and not be so willing to allow others to dictate the direction of it. The goal is to live carefully and strategically using the gifts of your logic and not relying on emotions to cloud your judgment. You will have a clear vision of what the *Free Agent Lifestyle* looks like.

Most men will struggle with this position. It is not what we are conditioned to believe regarding social interactions and relationships. We're told that there is one way; monogamy...or you'll be crucified (or even jailed) for living any other way but that. Most of you want a book on how to get more women and even fuck more women, as if it's some sort of mystery. You've tried it the exact same way with a few minor adjustments, but women still frustrate you. But this book will put you in the power position in every social interaction. The result may be that you get more and better quality women just by becoming interesting and being indifferent to them.

Most of the ideas in this book are information that your father should've told you. Or, maybe an uncle, or a cousin. But, even if your father thought to tell you these things, he was too weak to overcome the conditioning that told men to be silent. It still exists today, but people like me are saying, "Fuck it!"

I was never much of a coffee drinker. I've lived most of my life pretty clean, save for a few drinks here and there. I'm not a heavy drinker and I've never done any drugs, so I've always looked at coffee as one of those dependent chemicals that weak people use to keep themselves awake to do average stuff. But to finish this book, I drank a 'helluva' lot of coffee! I was training seven to eight people a day and making YouTube content and doing live streams, all while I was putting this book together. Work has never scared me. Considering the fact that seven years prior to writing this book, I was living in the back of my Ford Explorer after leaving my marital home, I'm in a better place.

When men choose to go their own way, one of the things that we face is shame and ridicule. We get blamed and criticized for making the decision to focus on ourselves. This is mostly because of what we take with it: the possibility of dates, the passing on of our resources for the possibilities of what could occur, the withdrawal from massive consumerism and even possibility of children and family.

Having a voice like mine is critical to the survival of many men. The social construct of relationships is being dictated by those who benefit the most from our compliance. If you speak against this construct, you get treated with hostility.

Shaming Language

Shaming language is either centered around emotions, or it's an attack on a man's masculinity. People who use shaming language rarely attempt to use logical argument to dispute the statistics that were provided to demonstrate the need for men to focus on themselves. Rather, the shaming comes in the form of gas lighting. Gas lighting is an abusive and manipulative tactic that some use to get you to question your own sanity. When I express my ideas about relationships and use statistical evidence to reference my ideas, instead of debating me with logic, women and even some men will make it seem like it's not real, that I'm the only one experiencing or imagining it. When people gaslight and use shaming tactics, it's a way to switch the subject to something else, to shift the blame to you rather than taking accountability for the real reasons I drew my conclusion. The idea or evidence is never addressed; rather, my sanity or masculinity becomes the conversation.

Examples of Gas lighting and shaming techniques:

"What kind of women are you meeting?" (As if they have never heard of anyone like that)

"Who hurt you?" (An admission that women behave poorly, but you should MAN UP and handle it)

"You must be gay!" (An attack on your masculinity; changes the subject to my sexuality rather than the original topic)

"You must be picking the wrong women?" (Questioning your ability to discern between good and bad people; not addressing the behavior of those people)

"You can't get the women that you want." (An attack on your masculinity or sexual marketplace value)

"You're just bitter." (Not addressing the issue or evidence, just your ability to handle poor behavior emotionally)

"You're too old and ugly..." (Attacking your sexual marketplace value, not the evidence or topic; attempt to change the subject by making it emotional, rather than logical)

"You hate women." (Bringing emotions into the argument, but not disputing the evidence)

I've been talking about men issues for many years and have heard these questions and statements more times than I could count. I used to address them, but after discovering that the gas lighting technique never really dealt with anything that I was talking about, I try to shift the conversation back to the subject. It usually ends the conversation or turns it into something reminiscent of a debate at a high school cafeteria table.

By the way, just because you're a *Free Agent* doesn't mean that you don't interact or sleep with women. You just don't prioritize them. You don't make them first in your life, without determining the value that they bring to you. You interact with them carefully and strategically. Never underestimate how much you can lose by choosing the wrong type of relationship.

Free Agent Women?

Can women live the *Free Agent Lifestyle*? The short answer is that they already do. In fact, women have been encouraged to be strong and independent for decades, thanks to feminism. When women choose to focus on themselves, get their money right or prioritize their dreams, they get praised. They have been told that if a man won't give them what they want, they can get it themselves. Women travel around the world on their own or travel in their "pseudo-Sex And the City" groups, and it's a big celebration of their independence. But, when men are encouraged to focus on themselves, travel on their own, to not be a pet wallet and provider for women, then here comes the guilt trip and shaming language.

The Mission

My mission is to be able to talk to as many groups of young men as possible. Primary and Secondary schools have girl empowerment seminars, sponsored by their school and women's groups all the time. These events are not even being taught during school hours! Why aren't young men being taught these things in school? It is time for men to receive information that can help and empower them. This lifestyle is not being presented as an option for men, neither are the pitfalls and traps that seem to impact men every year. It could save the lives of many young boys who are lost.

CHAPTER 1

THE MISTAKE

She sold me out for $500 a month in alimony and child support, sold my kids' names to the state to live off the government's dole and make me a debtor and possible prisoner of the state. That's how I look at the near $60,000 price tag of my divorce. At the end of the day, I was made the sacrificial lamb, the lean meat for the family courts to feast off of. If this were a legitimate business deal, it would be a colossal failure on any scale. A mistake, regardless of who was involved. I would have to give up everything that I knew because of this mistake.

Living in the back of my Ford Explorer would put things in perspective really quick. Nothing will make you dwell on your mistakes like stepping out of the back of your car at 3:00 AM to take a piss between the hedges that separates one parking lot from another. But, I was fortunate enough at least to have a car to live in. Many men who go through this phase don't even have that much.

Six months prior, I was the head women's basketball coach at a small Division II university in New Mexico. I now became a street dweller, trying to bounce back from my mistake. I had the biggest fight of my life in front of me, and everything from my kids to my fucking name was at stake. Why do these things have to be so petty?

When it comes to divorce, people want to play the blame game. The reality is that both people are at fault. No one is perfect in his or her marriage and the same could be said of my ex and I. While I don't like to place blame for this type of failure, I do hold someone responsible for what happens when a marriage ends. There should still be a level of respect, even in failed relationships. Using children as pawns and allowing the courts to weaponize the mother is unacceptable and unforgivable.

I'm not unique because I had a divorce; in fact, many men have gone through divorce before me, and many certainly will after me. Women file for divorce more than 80% of the time since the establishment of "no fault divorce" in the 1970's. They say that you never know a woman until you see her in family court. In my case, this shit is true. I can't even imagine that I spent a day in my life with this person. Who is she?

Spending 100 + days at the family court building over seven years can leave a foul taste in your mouth. Did it help lead me to the *Free Agent Lifestyle*? Yes, but this is just the tip of the iceberg. Let me explain.

It takes a lot of guts to speak about your divorce or breakup. There are many reasons that men stay silent about their divorce. There are not many avenues for men to express their thoughts and feelings. Specifically, for these reasons:

- It's too painful
- Courts forbid them from talking about it
- Fear that they will be perceived as weak for complaining
- They went to counseling to resolve the issue privately.
- They are censored or shamed by their friends on social media
- They just move on with life and figure that other men will find out for themselves.

I've always had the dream to be a *Free Agent* my entire life. After all of the accomplishments that I'd been able to achieve and the strategic planning of my life, I made a critical mistake. This mistake produced two tremendous gifts, but also gave me the worst years of my young life. This mistake, this decision, would cost me more than fifteen years of agony, and fifteen years of pain and stress. My children were the by-products of this mistake.

This mistake was a bit of a self-fulfilling prophecy, something that I've always felt would happen to me, but when it came true, living it brought absolute grief. It is the reason why I campaign so hard for men to live this lifestyle before they make a decision that could change their lives for the worse, more often than not. Often times, men who follow me who want to start families, ask me this question, "What if I want to have children?" "What if I want to leave a legacy behind, who do I leave it with?" I give them many options to bring children into the world. If a legacy is what they want to pass on, while at the same time, avoiding some of the agony associated with failed marriages, then it is vital that they explore ALL options associated with having children.

Most people think that they can only have children via a marital union. Statistically, this is the best way to raise children, but with the rate of divorce in our country, marriage is not the safest option. I mean, you cannot guarantee that you would stay married for longer than 10 years. In fact, the statistics reveals that you will more likely be divorced, split up, or alienated from your family, rather than being with them through your kids' entire childhood. This can make your time with your children limited and result in many painful meetings with attorneys, child support agents and judges.

Many men start to look for other ways that they can validate their own emotional importance or how they think about themselves.

Use Your Logic, Not Your Emotions

Most of the mistakes that we make in our lives are the result of us listening to our emotions and not thinking logically about things. People encourage you to do so with sayings like "Follow your heart" and "Love is the answer." However, that's the trouble with humans. Once their emotions are involved, they don't think very clearly. They end up making terrible mistakes that are only realized once the emotions are removed and your brain calculates the dumbness of your emotional decision.

With all of the information that we have and the statistics that are made available to us, choices like these should be easy to make. Yet, others encourage us to disconnect the statistics from the decision making process. These statistics didn't come from outer space. It is real data that should be interpreted and used to make judgments in order to prevent pain, hurt and financial loss. It is important that you ALWAYS use your logic and follow your thoughts.

Mistakes can bring positives as well as negatives. Make no mistake about it; I could never imagine my life without my children. I have worked tirelessly to ensure that they have the best options available to them. I have volunteered at their school and was even voted "father of the year" by the school's PTA board. The award was given to the father that contributed the most in terms of hours and resources to school. During that time, I was the vice president of the PTA and was the event coordinator for one the school's major fundraisers, the *Jog-A-Thon*. I was able to raise $120,000 over three years while heading the fundraiser. I'm very proud of this accomplishment.

All the while, my ex-wife was sabotaging my time and experience with my children, and she used every available resource that women are afforded by state agencies to do so. Other women saw it and sponsored it, while others looked the other way, choosing to not get involved.

Despite all of the bullshit, I stood up and fought for my children. I was vigilant and continued to volunteer at the school and to coach their sports teams so I could spend more time with them; time that my ex would usually use to keep my children away from me. Ultimately, I would get full custody of my children because the vindictive nature of my *baby mother terrorist* led her to make mistakes in the eyes of the family court. This victory meant the world to me, but the sad reality is that I wished I had never met her.

Stories like mine are not isolated incidences. In fact, as horrible as my story is, many men have shared far worse stories than mine. I've witnessed horrible custody battles where women believed that they owned the children and proceeded to torture and terrorize the father with the use of the archaic laws of the family court. This is why I encourage men to avoid the following mistakes.

Mistakes That You Want To Avoid

1. Cohabitation – Never move in with a woman

When I was in my teens, I had a male mentor who would talk to me about relationships. This mentor was not religious, which is important with regards to the guidance that he gave me, because a lot of religious men tend to have a battle between their logical position and the weak nature of the modern church. Religion today is very blue-pill oriented, but the words in the bible are not. With this confusion, the church began catering to women, homosexuals and mentally disturbed individuals and a lot of their doctrine can lead you right back into situations that you were trying to avoid with great logic and deliberation.

This mentor was in his 50's, he owned his own home, he never moved in with a woman, he didn't have children and he never married. This guy would give me advice on what to do in relationships. He told me to do all of these things except "Don't get married." I wish he would have told me that part as well; it would've saved my life.

However, he told me this rule: "Rule #1: Never Move In With A Woman." His point was that, if you're going into a relationships with a woman and you decide to live together, never be the one to move into her space. Because it will never be your space.

Now, most of us that have been in relationships and marriages, already know that even if you purchased a house, and even if you have all of the financial risk and responsibilities of the property, it's barely even your home when a woman lives with you.

The evidence of this is men who talk about having a "Man Cave" in their own home. Many times, this Man Cave is in the cold and dark recesses of the garage, unfinished basement or on the back patio area between the back yard and the house, where groups of men go out and grill meat and guzzle beer. The Man Cave is small place where he can carve out space from the home that he pays for which he can call his own. 90% of the rest of the house belongs to the wife and the children. Most women won't acknowledge this, but you can go into their bathroom's and see the pink toilet seat covers and pot pouri on the toilet tank. You can walk inside of their bedroom and see the twenty-eight different size pillows all over their bed. Even with that, she still will never admit that she is dominating the space.

Even in a situation where you let her move in with you, she will dominate that space. So imagine a situation where you move in with a woman and it was already her space to begin with and you are the last added piece to that space. How much of her space will she allow you? How much respect will she have for you if you've moved in with her? When that relationship goes bad, guess who is going to be the one who is put out on the curb with their bags and clothes spread out across the front lawn? It's gonna be you! You have no entitlements to that property and she will make sure that you wouldn't. That's why you don't appear on the lease and probably don't possess a mailbox key. You have no legal protection should she try to get you removed from the property during one of her emotional tirades.

A woman who moves in with a man will ensure that she has legal protections so you cannot spontaneously ask her to leave. She will make sure she is on the lease, has a mailbox key, receives mail at the residence, build relationships with neighbors so they can vouch for her residing there and push for engagement or marriage to secure her position (sign a state marital contract). She's going to make sure that she has some sort of dominion over that property via decorating the space or coercing you to move your filthy furniture out and purchasing half or more of the new furniture that she suggests. The amount of pillows will magically increase on your sofa and your bed.

The sad part is that men are too willing to give in to this because she has what he wants and he's too weak to take a stand against the person who rations out P-sleeve to him.

If a man moves into a woman's space, none of the entitlements that I mentioned above will be afforded to him, and he definitely is not getting a Man Cave in a property that she has dominion or legal rights over.

By the way, a Free Agent doesn't believe in Man Caves. The whole damn cave is our cave! We have dominion over our ENTIRE space.

2. Long Term Relationships (LTR's)

All long-term relationships end up in two ways; they either turn into a marriage or they end. There is no in-between. Rarely do you hear couples introduce someone as his or her girlfriend or boyfriend of 50 years. Hell, even a 15 year LTR is extremely rare. For LTR's that end, you've dodged a bullet. For LTR's that turn into marriage, you are now on track to becoming a statistic.

Today's women bring very little to the table and with the ability to get easy sex in our whorish culture, there is no need to commit to a woman nor do you want to commit to a person that has been doing monkey double backflips on the cock carousel for the past 12-15 years.

It must be understood that women who pursue LTR's are setting you up for the <u>next</u> commitment. They are temporarily satisfied with your initial commitment, but make no mistake about it; she will be pushing you into paying the ultimate price and laying down your life for her in short order. Marriage is always the goal.

Your time is too valuable to commit to a LTR at a young age. Much of this book will explain this point further, so let's skip to the next mistake to avoid.

3. Marriage

Despite the amount of men that have horror stories about the realities of married life and the statistical data that reveal the failure rate of marriages in the United States, some men feel that they are immune to these situation. They believe that it cannot happen to them, but what they don't understand is that everything is working against them to ultimately fail. Even a successful marriage doesn't look that great and if it is a colossal failure, it will affect you for the rest of your life.

Men who marry are usually in a bit of an orgasmic stupor and are following their lustful heart. They are listening to the words of a 20-year-old woman and don't understand that this person will not be the same person 10-15 years from now. They don't understand that they are forfeiting Peace, Quiet, and Freedom, and that their *Free Agent* status is forever withdrawn.

The real story is that seven out of ten marriages will end in divorce within ten years. This stat is available to everyone but people are afraid to look at it, just like they choose to ignore their bank account just a few days prior to their direct deposit hitting. Of course, your girlfriend knew this.

Did she discuss this with you? If she did, I'm sure she talked about how your love is like no other love and about how she would never be the type of person to drag you through a painful divorce and keep your children away from you. The statistics say otherwise.

Consider these statistics:

- Women file for divorce more than 80% of the time

- Women get full custody of the couple's children 83% of the time after a divorce

- Fathers with visitation or no custody are often alienated from their children

- The best-case scenario for custody (fathers) is 50/50, the worst case is 0%
  the best case for custody (woman) is 100%. The worst case is 50/50

- The average length of marriage for couples in their 20's: Eight years.

- 70-80% of women who have children experience postpartum depression after their first child. Those symptoms could last up to three years. This will effect your relationship in major ways.

- 20-30% of marriages are considered sexless marriages.

- If you stay married for more than 10 years, the wife may be entitled to LIFETIME alimony (depends on your states).

Unfortunately most men do not do their due diligence and research before making this life-long agreement. They take the leap of faith, again using their emotions rather than their logic. Too often, these stats can be discredited by these simple phrases from their future wives:

- "I would never do that."
- "Not all women are like that."

Just remember, that enough women ARE like that and that they are empowered by the state and backed by the state's weapons to turn your life upside down. Once you marry, the gun is placed to your head. Do as she says or you become a statistic!

The Other 50%

People often use the misleading 50% divorce rate to defend the success of marriage. We all know that the actual divorce rate is around 67%, but the thought process is that they are conceding to the narrative of 50% of marriages are unsuccessful and miserable, but the other 50% of marriages that survive are happy and successful. But, this graph will shred this theory into pieces. Admittedly, it is not scientifically valid, but the illustration is relevant because we all know many couples that fall into these categories, and although we know they exist, they are often not spoken about. The problem is that these couples are included in the so-called successful 50% of marriages, and that is problematic!

The graph shows that of the "Other 50%" that stayed married:

- 10% stayed for the children
- 10% fear divorce and the implications on the family
- 5% stayed because of the time invested
- 4% stayed for religious reasons
- 4% remained together due to family pressure
- 4% stay for financial reasons; can't afford divorce

- 4% remained together due to age; too old to divorce
- 4% were given false hope by marriage counselors and others
- 4% have low self-worth
- 1% were in happy, well-balanced marriages

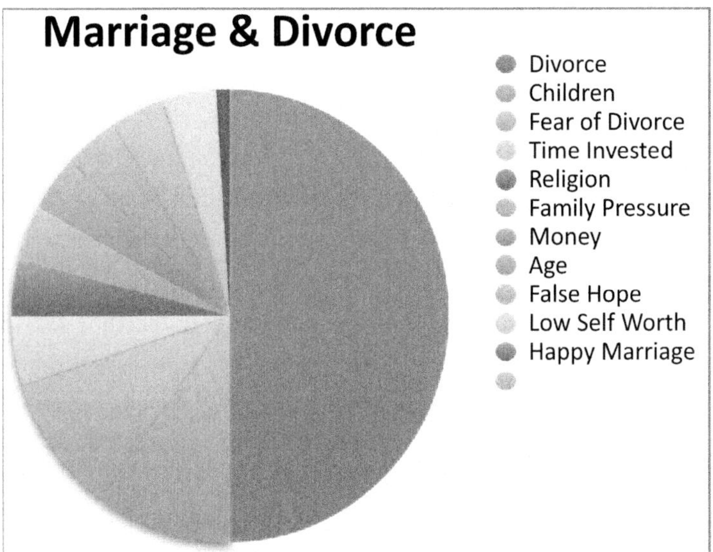

For those people who were in marriages that failed, some seek to re-marry, believing that it was the other person that failed rather than looking at the external factors such as feminism, which places a strain on the matrimonial home. They seek to correct their mistake by getting remarried, but 2nd and 3rd marriages have a divorce rate of 75%-90% and the statistics are worse when two divorced people decide to marry.

The reality is that there are not that many successful marriages where BOTH people are committed for the long haul. We also know that 20-30% of these unions are considered sexless marriages, meaning the couple engages in sex less than twice a month after ten years of marriage, and those sexual sessions can be chalked up to duty or pity sex. We also know that 55% of husbands report that they have had a sexual affair during their marriage while 50% of wives reports the same. Marriage for most, if not all, is a big mistake.

CHAPTER 2

FREE AGENT LIFESTYLE

The Tenets of living the Free Agent Lifestyle

- Keep yourself unchained

- You have little to no commitments to others. Keep your commitments low or preferably nonexistent.

- Free from debt and irresponsible spending – live minimally (student/consumer loan debt/housing debt)

- Freedom from banks (Banks will dip into your account at will and allow others to do so through court order, i.e., IRS, Child Support, etc.). They aren't offering much in terms of their usefulness, so be careful putting all of your money in there. The FDIC only insures $250,000.

- Keep your power to decide. Free Agency is about having options. When you are committed, you have way less options and/or you're doing the options of others.

- Limit your work commitments. If you can start your own business rather than working the slave 9-5 job, do it. It doesn't have to be a multi-million dollar business or something that controls you night in and night out. If you have a business that employs over 50 people, you become married to it, but I wouldn't be mad if you had one. If your ambition, drive and determination take you to that level, then by all means, do it! But, be aware that those type of business have a way of controlling your time, thoughts and clarity.

The Thought Behind the Free Agent Lifestyle

The *Free Agent Lifestyle* comes from the sports equivalent idea of free agency, where an athlete's contract has expired and they are eligible to freely sign with any club or franchise. This athlete is free to receive offers from other teams and other teams can use their best recruiting tools to solicit the services of the free agent since they are not bound to a contract.

Free Agency in sports is a fairly new concept. Prior to 1975, teams had a reserve clause in players' contracts, which stipulated that once the commitment term had expired, only that club had a right to re-sign the player. If they didn't want to sign the player, the player would have to secure a new deal with another team prior to the start of the season. This gave the player less leverage. With free agency, teams would know when a player's contract or commitment ended and it gave more options and power to the player.

Relationships and marriages should work the exact same way. There should be a term that both people agree to, let's say seven years, where the husband and the wife would give their best efforts. After the seven-year term, both are free to go their own way without penalty, to secure a better deal or to remain free. If they want to stay together, they can bind themselves under a longer term with whatever they agree to. This is using logic and subtracting the emotion from the decision. Unfortunately, those who benefit wouldn't want it this way, because "marriage is about love" right?

Throughout the years of watching sports, I discovered that the Free Agents held the most power. The power in deciding, in negotiating, and in recruiting. They have the ability to leverage their talents for more options and dollars from their old team or a new team. As a Free Agent's contract was set to expire, they received much less criticism than those who were under contracts/commitments.

The athletes that held the least amount of power were those who were under contract. If you're under contract, you have expectations and MUST meet them. You receive criticism if your performance isn't up to par and will be constantly reminded of your shortcomings. Think of the married men, who receive their honey-do list whenever the weekend arrives, they have their kid's sports commitments to attend, they have trips to the farmers market or the festival with their girlfriends, they have their girlfriend's or wife's family events, where they must show their happy face as they watch their little nephew Johnny smash his first cupcake all over his high chair. Those are some of the expectations that they must meet or the woman who is setting these expectations might get her feelings hurt. You spend most of your weekend trying to manage her emotions by becoming a dancing monkey. She might not give you any P-Sleeve if she gets upset, so you must do those all of these things AND with a smile. Or else, criticism is the next weapon she will use against you. If you're not doing it the way that she wants, then your performance is criticized.

Free Agents don't have those expectations to meet. They've already proven themselves worthy of receiving the best offer at any time, without criticism. Every weekend, you get everyone's best performance. Every outing, you get to decide what you're doing and if you want someone to do it with. Or, preferably doing something solo and enjoying it! That is, until you commit. Most of the time, all Free Agents receive is praise from those who seek your commitment. If someone's offer is less than quality, or not up to your standard, then you can walk away and lose nothing. A committed player cannot do the same.

There is always a need for Free Agents. There is always a drive to get you on someone's team because you are more attractive when you show value than when you are committed. As a Free Agent you don't have to be on anyone's team. You can choose to make your own path and play by your own rules. You can choose to go your own way.

The *Free Agent Lifestyle* is not just talking about relationships; however, relationships are the area where most men make their biggest mistakes. *Free Agent Lifestyle* also talks about work, recreation, health, making the right economic decisions for your personal self, talking care of your children (if you've already been through the divorce grinder), and the importance of self-care.

Men who take this approach get a lot of shaming because they are taking back the control of their lives, and are not allowing outside forces to control them. This lifestyle is a major threat to many. If it wasn't, no one would care if we went our own way. But, they care! They get upset like they are losing something. They know that once you decide to be a Free Agent, they cannot extract resources from you based on an emotional connection or contract. You are always bringing logic to the discussion and they can't manipulate your logic, can they?

Jobs – Just Over Broke

Listen, you have to do what you have to do to make ends meet and support yourself. But, do you have to give your time away to soul crushing "jobs"? Can you start your own business or become an independent contractor? That's something you would have to explore for yourself.

We all need to work, but we don't need to take years off of our lives so we can make a comfortable salary and keep us working just enough to eat for another month. Start your own business. Be self-employed, develop a side hustle or turn a skill into income. Become an investor. Whatever you can do to free yourself and earn money, instead of making someone else rich, do it!

I have been self-employed for the past seven years. Prior to that I was a salary-earning college basketball coach for 15+ years. I thought coaching was my dream job, but working as a private trainer where I eat what I kill is something like heaven. I don't work for a gym, I work independently, I do my own marketing, obtained my own clients and I go to my clients instead of having the clients come to me. I have very little overhead and best of all, I set my own schedule, price and standards.

It would have been easier to just get a job with a gym and let them market my name within their business structure, but I would have to accept the crumb rates that they pay their trainers. To make what I make as an independent trainer, I would have to work double the hours and that's not physically possible. Sure, building my own clientele was harder. It took three years of eating plates of shit to get consistent business. But, after the hard climbing and dedication to promoting myself, it was the best decision for my life. Those three years are in the past, and I'm in full control of my life. I'm my own boss!

People believed that my goal was to own a gym. But, even this idea was limiting my freedom. The thought of owning a gym was NEVER my goal or intention. In fact, working as a full-time trainer was not my passion. My passion was supporting my children and living my life. Owning a gym required managing employees and front desk staff, ordering and maintaining equipment, organizing class schedules, leasing space, collecting rent from trainers, managing payroll and developing marketing ideas and cattle calls to get more clients through the door. I had absolutely NO interest in that. I would have no freedom with that setup.

Find something that works for you and that provides you a level of freedom that allows you to enjoy your life. Don't be lazy because I said to not have a job. In fact, you should be working to develop more streams of income so you can be a true Free Agent. Especially when you're young! In 10 years, you can set up enough income streams that can literally pay you while you're sleeping. Or, better yet, while traveling!

This is where you want to get to achieve the ultimate goal: Peace, Quiet, and Freedom.

Focus On the Things That Matter

Soon, you will discover that the P-Sleeve doesn't matter in the long run. Sure, it brings you pleasure temporarily. But, if you focus on it, it will control you. You become a classic dick thinker or a panty collector, someone who equates sticking body parts into others as an achievement. To become Free Agents, we have to start thinking with our big head, instead of with our little head.

We are extremely fortunate to be living this life. It's a miracle that your sperm was the one that won the race to your mother's egg. But always remember that this is not a dress rehearsal. You are not living the practice life for the life that you want to live the next time you're here. This is it! We ain't coming back! This is the one life that you're going to get, so get everything out of it that you can.

We must think past the point of being providers for individuals who don't appreciate or value us other than using us to obtain the things that they cannot get on their own. They see us more as resource providers than as partners. Ultimately, they have the power to use systems that are provided by the state's government to extract those same resources from you, should you choose to not toe the line.

There are other things that you could be doing with your time. Focus on getting your money right. Start reading and focus on bettering yourselves for the life that you can provide for yourself instead of bettering or improving yourself for women.

By becoming a Free Agent, we're not bettering ourselves for women to date. We're not bettering ourselves to meet society's expectations. We're not bettering ourselves to become better mates and providers for others. We're putting our best foot forward for ourselves!

There is real power in your commitment. And, your commitment transfers that power from you to the person you give it to. If you give your commitment away too easily without showing value, they will not respect you in the end. At that point you are disposable and can be replaced if needed. This is why you shouldn't commit to anyone unless you can demonstrate high value. Then you can be more selective and have more options to pick from, and in return, that person will be more appreciative of your efforts and you have a higher likelihood of them respecting you. You want these individuals giving you their best effort at all times!

THIS is my passion: To see brothers getting better without the struggle of dragging someone along for the ride. You can only get better when you're focusing on yourself. Not by focusing on others, or on P-sleeve, or dating. Focus on yourself, first. You can't do it when you're focusing on ass and titties, and returning messages on the online dating cesspool. Focus on what matters, no matter what.

No Long Term Relationships / No Cohabitation / No Marriage

We have been indoctrinated into believing that pair bonding is our only option and the type of lifestyle that we must desire above all others. The fact is that you can be happy and remain single, you can have multiple girlfriends, you can date non-exclusively with no commitment, be polyamorous, whatever suits YOU. Sure, there are dangers to any lifestyle that you choose but Free Agents are able to choose for themselves. However, being sold the idea that marriage is your only choice for happiness is irresponsible and the sellers of marriage are not looking out for you, they are looking out for everyone except you.

When it is sold this way, people rush out to do it without doing their due diligence on how it will negatively affect them, in the event that it does not work. We know that marriage does not work for most, if not all people. Well, neither does co-habitation or long term monogamous relationships. People are cheating on each other, ALL THE TIME!

Yes, society benefits from marriage and monogamous relationships, but at the expense of the individual. We are sold on the benefits: child raising, loyal sexual partners, financial stability, home ownership in safe suburbs, etc., but those benefits aren't even guaranteed. Just look at the divorce rate and the amount of children being raised in co-parenting or single parent homes.

People are HOPEFUL about the benefits but when Free Agents discover that it does not work, we are discouraged from protecting ourselves from the failure rate. Pre-Nuptial and post nuptial agreements, which are designed to protect men and their assets from losses in failed marriages, are deemed unfair by those who would benefit if the marriage fails. But it is only fair to protect yourself and what you've worked hard for, so if they don't want to play by your rules, then stay FREE.

Think about the housing market in the early 2000's and the collapse and foreclosure mess that people got themselves into because everyone was sold on the idea of pride of homeownership and the ease of purchasing homes with those creative financing programs. Most, if not all of these companies failed and failed big, because people bit off more than they could chew. I look at marriage and relationship through the same lens. Like houses in 2004, they are easy to get in, but hell to get out of. We are sold on the happiness, the emotions, the sexual exclusivity and enjoyment of the first six months, but once that wears off, you're left with two humans that have to deal with reality in their own little nest. The housing market collapses ruined people's credit, led to people losing their homes, drove home prices up across the country and led to massive unemployment in certain areas. Similarly, divorce and breakups have the same effect, but on a more personal level; ruining your credit or financial standing, separating children from parents and causing children to live their lives in suitcases and backpacks until the age of 18. People need to get real about relationships and marriage and stop hoping for the best and start doing the best for themselves. Hope is not a strategy!

These are things that no one wants to discuss openly and when I do it, they just ignore me or shame me. They don't look at the numbers;

they look at what they can gain emotionally and financially from men's stupidity. They want to live in their fantasyland, but don't want to address it until it affects them. They act surprised at the outcome, but we should be made aware of these outcomes far in advance. We are smarter than these people, but we chose to stay dumb.

CHAPTER 3

DON'T BOX YOURSELF IN

Part of the attraction to the *Free Agent Lifestyle* is that you have the ability to go and grow at any time, and to any level. The sky is the limit or as Michael Jordan says; "the ceiling is the roof." LOL

But, all jokes aside, if there was one piece of advice that I would tell my younger self, it's this: Don't box yourself in too young. Avoid getting into relationships too young, too fast.

Listen, some of the things that we are looking to gain out of relationships are children, companionship, the ability to pass on our legacy to our offspring and sexual exclusivity with women who has a small sexual history. Most of these things can happen at ANY time a man's life. We can be 50-60 years old when this occurs. If we've taken care of our health, our bodies, and our business, we would have far more things to pass on to our children, with a lot more energy to do so. Humans are living much longer than we've ever have in our existence so there shouldn't be a rush to create this.

In fact, you can create this family at an older and wiser age, and have a far better experience with a better family situation than we would if we start off younger. I know, no one is promised tomorrow, but if you died before age 50 then, you would've missed a part of it anyway and passed on very little to your children to begin with.

Unfortunately, our emotions and our dicks control us. Our little head overpowers the big head for men and the heart controls the minds of women. In our teenage years, the hormones kick in and we have the biological need to procreate. But, the world is not prepared for two young people to bring in a child any longer. There is a case for an older man and a younger woman (of legal age of course) to bring in a child, but that's another discussion for another book.

In our urge to mate and procreate, we often make choices as young people that will drastically affect our lives and ability to enjoy that life. Men marry too young, have children too young and end up pigeon holing themselves in careers and trades at a young age just to support the family. We get into situations like this before we can understand them.

If you make a commitment too early and tie yourself down, you may be closing the doors to opportunities in the future. Forget what women are trying to sell you about building something together. That's pure nonsense. When I was married, I saw wives doing things that were more debilitating to men and their ambition than they were helpful. The fear of taking risks overtook them, as well as the lack of quality time, the need for attention and the careful distribution of financial resources. Thus, many families struggled longer than necessary. They missed opportunities to travel because of tight budgets and work commitments. Also, because the children were too young to travel. They missed opportunities because they were tied down with a mortgage and couldn't relocate in time to take advantage of that opportunity. The reality is; you can always get married, you can always buy a house, but you cannot always recreate opportunities.

When I got separated and divorced, I met women who were way better human beings that my ex-wife and would've made far better wives. But, at the time I was selecting my wife at a young age, I overlooked obvious red flags and had a scarcity mindset, believing that I would never find another one like her. But, that is false!

Staying free willed makes you more valuable. You will be free to do things that others, who tied themselves down, cannot do because they committed too early.

The biggest thing you can give a woman is your commitment. With that commitment, you are taking yourself off the market and committing time, money and energy to her and everything that comes as a result of your union. You can no longer pursue opportunities without her compliance. She now holds all the power in your relationship, because she has the ability to say yes or no to decisions that you could have easily made on your own. When you're free, you have the ability to do things and make her wait on you.

Areas to Avoid Boxing Yourself In

When you avoid boxing yourself in, you are protecting yourself from making bad decisions. I speak about relationships a lot but there are other ways that you can box yourself in. Let's take a look at them:

Job/employment

In our society, everyone is very career focused. The reality is that most people don't have careers. They have a series of jobs that they jump back and forth to, in order to make ends meet. Hell, NFL players have an average career span of three seasons. After the games end, they are still young and have to find work.

When I was starting off my "career" as a college basketball coach, a mentor that helped get me in the business told me, "you shouldn't spend more than five years at any job. You make yourself less valuable by sticking around at a company. They know your strengths and weaknesses, they know your personal problems and they know that you'll stay committed to them no matter what." In fact, promotion from within is much slower than having the ability to sell YOURSELF to a new company and get hired quicker and at a higher level. This does depend on your company's culture, but this is generally true. It is the reason why you see new people get hired at levels higher than yours and you get pissed when that happens.

The way your company sees it is that you're still here, you haven't left yet, so what's the rush in promoting you. They can promote you much slower, give you crumbs and still get something out of you at lower costs. If there were ever a reason why the gender wage gap exists, this would be an antidote or explanation as to why it exists. Women tend to stay at companies and wait to get promoted. This is a less-risk, less-reward mindset. This leads to lower wages and a lesser ability to negotiate better wages. Overtime, the company begins to devalue you but your best asset is your experience. Take the experience with that company and offer it to another business, perhaps a competitor and they will pay you accordingly. Sticking with one way to do things does not make you valuable to that same company. Companies are looking for solutions, not parrots. Every company loves team players, but in sports, team players get paid less than the stars. You need both stars and team players to win, so why not be the star. CEO's make moves all the time! Why should you stay and lose.

The ultimate strategy is to take the experience that you learned on your company's time and start your own business. Even riskier, but the rewards are limitless. Maybe you become a competitor or maybe you offer something that your current employer needs and they can hire you at a consultant rate. If you haven't signed a non-compete clause, you can become a competitor right away.

Why limit yourself? You must have an abundance mindset in regard to your life and trust in your ability. Some of you guys don't believe that you can get great things out of your life. You'd rather aim low and hit than to aim high and miss. You can be everything you see other people being. All it takes is belief and the ability to manage risks.

Some of you don't believe that you could be a billionaire! There are over 3000 billionaires in the world, why can't you be one. Jeff Bezos started Amazon at the age of 27 and it took some time and commitment to get it to the company that it is today. And today? He's the richest person in the world. Of course, his impending divorce will cost him that ranking. Looks like he boxed himself in on another level.

It is never too early to think about getting the type of income that you want in order to live the life that you want. Don't be afraid to dream big. Think about that number that you want to have and quadruple it. Or, like Grant Cardone says, "10X it!" Don't set your goal so low. Think about setting your goals very high with stages in between. If you set it high and miss by a little, it's better than setting your goal low and hitting it.

And this is important: Don't let age restrict or limit you. My son is always working on business ideas and I'm having him create business plans that will support the success of his ideas. Hopefully, this will help him understand his power and determination at a young age so that he can achieve a level of success that satisfies him at a young age. This thinking could change his life!

Real Estate

Buying a home at an early age can seem like a good idea. It seems like a good investment and it might be for some. I will preface any further advice now and tell you that I am a licensed realtor in my state and have studied real estate and trends. I have been a part of teams that have sold billions of dollars in property in one year. I also worked as a mortgage loan officer for 18 months between 2005 and 2006. If anyone remembers this time period, it was the beginning of the end for the great housing market crash and the massive foreclosures that affected us for many years. I have seen some critical mistakes in this area. I will admit that I am no expert, but I want to get you to understand my philosophy on this. This subject is where I get the most bite back from the pro-homeowner types.

I have seen people miss out on opportunities because they

couldn't sell their home fast enough to run through an open door. Or maybe they were upside down on the mortgage and it didn't make sense to sell it, so they decided to pass up on a brilliant opportunity.

Buying a home is a nice thing to add to your portfolio, but many people consider a home as an investment rather than just a place to live. They get consumed about the price and the market fluctuating instead of enjoying the home for what it is, four walls and a roof. If you want to invest in real estate, there are much better ways to do so. Boxing yourself in and pouring all of your money into one home is not the best way to get a return on your investment.

Other ways that may be better include; investing in four-plexes, gentrified neighborhoods, multiple single family residences (SFR) in small towns, apartment buildings and hotels. All of these have multiple residences, and if a tenant moves, your income does not end. You just have to replace one tenant, while the others continue to pay their rent. You can rent a nice home that you really like and live off the rest from your income producing properties. Listen, I can go on and on about this subject, but I'd rather refer you to Grand Cardone or Robert Kiyosaki's books than to hammer this point home.

If you already have boxed yourself in with a family and children then you are already stuck. Your wife will push you to purchase a home because of the safety and security that she needs. But, buying a home will make you less flexible. It could be a limiting factor between you and opportunity. The key things to remember is that there are more options available to you in real estate than purchasing a SFR.

Unfortunately, properties are sold to us as an emotional investment, just like love, relationships, and college. Commercials that are made by banks sell the emotion of the purchase, rather than the logic of it, and the bank benefits. Once again, someone always benefits when you stop thinking logically and make major decisions about your life with your emotions.

Instead of spending all of your money on a mortgage, furnishings from the Restoration Hardware, and spending your weekend afternoons at a Home Depot, mixing paint, how about living minimally, learning to invest in income producing properties and spending your time relaxing instead of working for the home you've purchased.

If you're a young man, with no family, children, wife or kids, why do you need 3000 sq. feet of nest? Especially when you have a limited amount of resources. If an opportunity comes up in another country, city or state, you're already a slave to your house and cannot move. You've boxed yourself in. You have plenty of time to settle down later. But not when you're young. By the time you sell your property, the door that was open to you would no longer be open. There are houses everywhere on this planet, why lock yourself into one so early?

If you've lived in a property for less than five year and you're making payments, odds are that you have not even touched your principal when you send your mortgage payment to the bank. You've just paid interest. If you sold that home today, you will likely take a loss, especially after paying real estate agent commission fees. Odds are that your property hasn't built up a considerable amount of equity to counter the amount loss, unless you've purchased in an area like southern California.

If you're a young man under the age of 32, without children and a wife, re-consider buying property in an area, where it will be your sole place of residence.

Don't own just one door.

Race

Believe it or not, we are 99% similar to the next man regardless of our skin color. We all share similar DNA and traits. What differentiates us is our culture.

Despite what the race baiter wants you to believe, we are more similar than we are different. We come from the same ancestors and if you think you are pure bred or anything, go get one of those ancestral DNA kits and you'll find out that your family tree contains groups of people that you've hated based solely on their skin color.

With the amount of wars and soldiers invading countries and raping, mating, and pillaging the women, and the amount of imperialism and interracial dating in the past 3000 years, to believe that you are pure bread at this point in history is ridiculous. The reality is, WE ARE ALL SIMILAR. But, for some reason when it comes to race, we are willing to box ourselves in. From what we believe, to the food we eat, to the music we listen to, we make decisions about our lives because of our skin color. If we listen to music or speak a certain way that is considered different from those who look like us, we get ridiculed, called names like sell-out, Uncle Tom or race trader. Even the lifestyle we chose to live, the activities that we participate in, the area we choose to live, the clothes that we wear, the people that we date or the sports team we cheer for can bring on a barrage of shaming language that is manipulative and controlling. It begins to get ridiculous! A Free Agent could care less about things like race, or restricting ourselves to those beliefs. Sure, we can celebrate our heritage and culture, but there's no benefit to us to restrict our lives based on it.

Some people are afraid to move from certain areas because of barbers and hair stylist that they're dependent on or the lack of similar people living there. Even if that area is a cesspool, they will live there as opposed to living in a safer community under the guise of sticking around and helping those who refuse to or cannot help themselves.

It's the easiest way to box yourself in, and actually the worst way, simply because you have no control over it. You have no control on how light or dark your skin is, neither do you have control over the fact that your hair is coarse and curly, or thin and straight. But we spend too much time and energy boxing ourselves in on things that we have little to no power in changing. You had no choice, your parents made that choice for you.

Why make decisions based on things that you had no choice in creating? Some things may happen to you based on how you look, but again, those are things you cannot control, so why put so much emphasis on your ONE LIFE based on the complexion of your skin? It makes no sense.

Relationships

Don't give your commitment away so easily. Nothing will take away your freedom faster than this. If you get married, you're a slave to her and her thoughts. If you knock her up, you're a slave to her and the state.

Guys, women will come and go. I always wish they'd come and go as fast as possible, but don't get one-itis over a pretty face. There are nearly 8 billion people on earth. You will meet a lot of women in your life.

The blue-pillers will shame you and claim that you'll be lonely. But, getting married will not guarantee that you will live a life that is not lonely. Look at the divorce rate. Look at the amount of people that live with sexless marriages after ten years. Look at the amount of married couples that live in separate bedrooms and are essentially roommates. They will tell you that you'll die alone. Well, unless you're in a bus full of people that travels over a cliff and explodes, odds are you're going to die alone.

If you prevent yourself from getting into these situations, you will have more control of your life than anyone wants you to have. They don't want you to be free. They don't want you out there unattached. They get nervous when you pull away from "the Matrix." Who are they? They are anyone who benefits from your resources and emotions being pulled into families, homes, racial strife and jobs.

CHAPTER 4

GOING SOLO

DOING SH*T ON YOUR OWN, ON YOUR OWN TIME

I don't know about you, but I find it absolutely amazing, the amount of times that I hear people say that they are surprised that I travel alone or even go to the movies by myself. It's as if I am supposed to be embarrassed to be seen doing things without other people. That shit never phased me.

I often found it interesting that when a man wants to do something, he feels the need to do it with a woman or a friend. He couldn't be seen doing it by himself. God forbid someone would think he was a loser for showing up to the movies without a date.

Interesting enough, I've always felt that attending a movie or a sports game was the worst dating idea ever. You're distracted! You go to a game to cheer on your favorite team, but if you go with a date, you're sitting on your hands so you don't appear overly passionate about your team. You're less likely to chant "Go Team," when the crowd starts yelling, you're less likely to join the wave, so you sit there looking too cool in front of the date that you're trying to impress. You miss three innings of the baseball game trying to get snacks at the concession stand only to return to your seats and find a couple of dudes spittin' game at your date.

One of the truths about me preferring to do things alone is that I'm extremely impatient when it comes to waiting on other people. Let's say an event starts at 7pm and I'm with a girlfriend and we are picking up other people to take to the event. Not only do I have to get ready and wait for my girlfriend to get her hair right, I calculate the drive time to pick up the other couple, and then hope that they're as ready as they need to be when I get there. Most of the time, their asses ain't ready, and I have to sit around, small talking while some woman fixes her hair just right. ARGGHHH!

Adding to that frustration, I have a need to be punctual, so making plans to go with multiple people is just not appealing to me.

I'm a social person and I don't mind spending time chopping it up, but I always apply the law of diminishing returns to these interactions. It doesn't seem necessary to spend 4-5 hours of a beautiful evening small-talking and chit-chatting. At some point it's fun, but after two hours, the evening dips into the "*WTF* am I doing here?" territory.

Another factor that contributes to my version of the *Free Agent Lifestyle*, is that I feel a lack of control when I'm not able to leave an event when I'm good and ready. I can't stand sitting around and waiting for other people to wrap up their conversations. During my teenage years, my mother would drag me to her church functions and social parties where she was enjoying the company of her friends, while I would rather be picking out my eyelashes than sitting and listening to their conversations. It wasn't that I didn't like the people; it was just not what I wanted to be doing. The absolute worst part of the evening was, instead of leaving when everyone else left, she would stay after and help clean the entire house before we left. It was a respectable things to do, but to have a teenage son waiting around for this was not respectful of my time or needs. At the point where I could drive my own car, I knew that I wouldn't put myself in a position to be driven to an event when I could just drive myself. My answer to "Should I meet at your place and we can drive over?" was always "No, I'll meet you there."

Even if I was the driver, I didn't want the responsibility of driving other people back from the event because they might want to stick around, talking well after the event. Fuck that shit! I'm out when I want to be out.

I don't even like to make a grand exit from a party. I don't feel the need to draw attention to myself as I'm leaving. I love to dip out quietly and unnoticed.

When it comes to relationships though, the overriding factor of going solo is that it's a helluva lot cheaper to do things alone than to bring a woman with you. If I am put in the position to pay for my entertainment AND hers, there is just no fair exchange in nearly every circumstance. I support paying for a person's time, that's what service providers are for. A fair exchange of time and money. Dates, wives and girlfriends actually get dates, trips and concert tickets paid for and men still have to be an emotional tampon, organize details within the event (dinner reservations and ideas, transportation, etc.) AND pay for everything that comes with it. All in the hope of getting some P-sleeve at the end of the night. This could go on for HOURS! And, the majority of the time, you get back home early the next morning too tired to even f*ck her brains out. You've worn yourself out trying to entertain her. Or, she gets a belly ache from all the dinner and entertainment that you've provided, so she's not much of a willing performer at 2am. Or, she gets sloppy drunk and less appealing and you've put yourself in the bull's eye for catching a #metoo case.

When you tally everything up, you've paid double for something and got less enjoyment out of it when you could've gone by yourself and enjoyed every minute of it.

When you go solo to events that you're passionate about, you actually meet other people that share your interest. Sharing an experience with people that understand the passion that you have for something brings additional gratification. You expand your circle and you get to be raw in your conversations with them. You get to share your knowledge about the subject and learn something that will help you in the long run.

If you're caught up into trying to bring dates to these type of events, she's probably not going to have genuine interest in doing these things, but may go along for the ride because it is no cost to her, plus she still gets validation and attention. But, trust me, she is taking notes about certain things, and will be ready to pass judgment on you when the things works for her.

To avoid this, men will end up choosing things for her entertainment and less for his own. Worse still, they pay double to do some shit that they would've never done in their own free time.

When you go to these events solo, it often takes less time, less planning, and you're less rushed. You will find new discoveries about things that may interest you because you are giving them more attention, plus you're not listening to someone else distracting you, you're not focused on trying to look cool and you're not just trying to get to the end of the evening so you can attempt to bang her brains out.

If you're stuck thinking of things to do solo, consider the list below and some of the benefits of going by yourself:

Traveling

Don't get one-itis for the location that you live. Break up the monotony and travel. Get your passport, buy a ticket, get a map or hire a tour guide and see how big the world is.

Through my time as a college basketball coach, I've been able to travel to every state in the United States with the exception of one. I'll let you guess which one it is (hint: it begins and ends with the same letter).

Once you're able to experience other areas and other cultures then you can come back to yours with a level of respect but an understanding that there are other people and other ways to live in a world other than what you have become accustomed to. $1000 can take you just about anywhere.

Going to the movies

The cost to go to a movie is downright crazy and having someone tag along can eat at your budget and prolong the evening unnecessarily. Besides, when you're watching a movies you're sitting in a dark room in silence. Why do you need someone else to be there with you? A movie is the worst dating idea unless you're in high school, when it's just an excuse to have a private "feel up" session in the only place you can find privacy. Hit the Sunday matinee or the theater that plays the cheap movies from six months ago and call it a day. You might have to experience sticky floors or wear a hoodie to sit in their seats, but you don't have to drag a two hour movie into a five-hour dinner, movie, and entertainment event.

Going to dinner

This is so underrated. Treat yo'self! Go to your favorite steak house and have dinner for one. Order a glass of your favorite joy juice, a nice, thick and juicy steak, and enjoy it in PEACE. You can get out under $50-$60 bucks, but you could triple that if you take a date with you. The crazy part is that men will take a woman to dinner at a high end place that he would never even consider treating himself to. Over-spending will fuck up your lifestyle real fast.

Going to concerts / concert in the park (free)

A friend of mine was dating a girl that loved Tim McGraw and this monkey simp bought her front row tickets to one of his shows. The entire evening, he told me how cold and distant she was with him, but how enamored she was with Tim from those great seats that he bought. Why do men do this to themselves? You don't provide opportunities like this to people that you date. She has no skin in the game, but you're burning a hole in your pocket trying to give her the royal treatment. Buy a ticket and go by yourself and enjoy the show instead of trying to impress a woman and spending the entire night trying to get close to her, only to be shut down. That's a heavy price to pay only to get rejected. Grab your blanket and hit the free concerts in the park during the summer and you might meet other people that share in your interest for music. A much better use of your time and resources and a better experience overall.

Going to sporting events

Taking women to a sporting event is a horrible idea. If you don't have front row tickets and you're sitting in the nose bleeds she will spend the entire night being jealous of the women that are in the lower bowl and wondering how she can get a man that has those seats. Besides, if you like the team, you can't really be yourself and cheer (or heckle) now, can you? Tickets with a date in the nosebleeds: $150. Tickets by yourself in the lower bowl, closer to the game: $150.

Going to the gun range

Let's say that a woman's views on gun laws and responsible gun ownership don't align with yours. She's intimidated by what those mean old nasty conservatives think about those dangerous guns.

Going to the gun range is extremely liberating and I have taken many men who had never shot a gun before mainly because their wife thought firearms were dangerous and they didn't want to make her uncomfortable. What is this world coming to? Go by yourself! Fuck what she thinks.

Going to the RC car park

The issue that you have to deal with is that your hobbies are not in line with her thinking. She may think that you're juvenile in pursuit of this hobby, but many times, if you go to an Remote Control car park, you will find men of all ages, men working alongside their sons, teaching skills on how to deal with problems that occur on the track with the car, making repairs, going through trial and error situations, and just bonding with their sons. She may call you a loser for taking part in a toy hobby, but the alternative of pursuing this hobby is spending time listening to her over a 12-15 hour non-stop talking, going shopping, planning trips that will cost you money, and drinking wine just so you can placate her. Now, which sounds more appealing? You make the call?

Going hunting, fishing or camping

This is where peace, quiet, and freedom lives. On a bass boat in the middle of a lake, in your travel trailer or tent at the camp site or in the woods, hunting and getting close to nature, and it's not a place to be getting sh*t tested or distracted. Unless you're linked up with a woman who actually enjoys these activities, do NOT take one with you. You will regret it.

Going to the observatory, museum, etc.

Let's get some culture in our lives brothers. Most men have never been to these places except on the first two or three dates with a woman. If you are bored or need to put your mind somewhere else, hit the art gallery, museum, or a theatrical performance and learn something new. Why not go by yourself?

Going to a CON (convention) event

There are many hobby conventions that travel across the country where you can meet people that you follow on social media or where you can purchase some of your favorite collectables. You can pretty much nerd out. Seek out events like Fitness Expos, Comic Cons, Vid Cons and even Porn Cons that will bring you closer to the people that you admire.

Be a Master of Your Own Schedule

Nothing comes between your hobbies and the shit that you need to get done. Never feel pressured to give up anything that you want to do just to give someone else attention. Remember, some people cannot receive enough attention; it is a bottomless pit and she waiting at the top to watch you attempt to fill it up. And, what you sacrificed last week means nothing this week. All of the effort that you put into filling it halfway does not matter. You have to start from the bottom the next week.

It's time to drop the dead weight in your life. Do you find yourself working hard to figure out a way to support more than yourself? People are quietly making this decision on their own, but they didn't have a label put on this lifestyle choice.

This is the Free Agent Lifestyle, where you take control of your schedule, your interests, and your life. You make your life about what you want to do, not what others want you to do for them. If they're interested in you, you set your own pace and let them catch you if they can

CHAPTER 5

RULES OF ENGAGEMENT

The dating game is rigged. Most of the time you hear someone talking about dating, you hear mostly negatives. Even if you get sex from the date, the process is just not worth it. Not only that, it's just not fun for men.

After a woman goes on a date, her friends will ask her how it went. They want the details; where they went, what plans he made, what they did, how his personality was, where they went to dinner, among other things. Most importantly, whether she had fun or not.

After a man goes on a date, his friends will want to know one detail: whether or not he had sex with his date or not. For men, the fun is not the date; the fun comes after the date. Everything he does leading up to the end of the date usually requires an excessive amount of work and effort and more often than not, he does not get to the "fun" part. On these dates, if a man expects "fun," he is considered a jerk. The main point to understand is that men who do not have sex after a date, or at least, kissing/making out/heavy petting, usually is disappointed with the evening's experience. I have yet to hear a man talk about all the fun he had organizing, planning, paying for everything, listening to some stranger give a five-hour wrap up of her childhood, education, career aspirations, past dates or relationships, followed by a visit to PornHub. Shit don't sound like fun, does it?

Men are finding it hard to balance treating women like equal, strong and independent ladies, and meeting the traditional expectations that Ms. Independent has set for you. I mean, we still have not answered the question of "who pays for the first date?" and we've been asking it for thirty freakin' years! Women aren't relenting, but they are finding it increasingly difficult to find eligible suitors. Hmmm, I wonder why.

The shallowness of today's women is hard to digest. Being judged on our physical prowess and ability to provide resources, while at the same time being shamed for having standards for women is a bit contradictory. A woman can freely ask for a man's height on a dating app, which is beyond his control, but men are shouted down if they ask for a woman's dress size or scale weight (which is something that they have full control over). Men are fed up with the double standards and hypocrisy, and are opting out. The worst part is that women aren't apologizing. But based on the principles of evolution, it is what it is.

Although I have been shunned and been turned down by many women based on my physical appearance, there have been many women who have overlooked it and that treated me like a prize. Admittedly, men can get greedy. We talk about those who don't like us, but forget those who do desire us for who we are. However, not many men have these options.

The #metoo movement has been a lesson in the disturbing behavior of women and their lack of agency and unwillingness to take accountability for their actions. I mean, women lobbing claims at men of means over bad dates that can't be proven or disproven and many times her poor judgment led to everything that she suggested happening. These events happened over 40 years ago, which opens men up to be targets on events that happened yesterday for many years forward. What's to say that a woman who experienced a bad date with a relatively poor man today can't target that man for a payoff twenty years later when he enters his prime earning years? The climate for engaging and associating with women is dangerous today and even 20-30 years from now.

The women who complain about online dating don't complain

about not getting matched, they complain about not being matched with those that they desire.

Women hate good men

Women have often asked the question, "Where have all the good men gone?"

Women are supposed to be the individuals who are making the right decision for their long-term benefit. Unfortunately we live in a feminist society and a whore-ish culture that promotes the fact that women can whore themselves out during their most fertile years then, at the last minute, find a good man to provided them with the house, the children, and the financial stability that they are entitled to. These are the "good men" that they are referring to. In reality though, they don't actually like good men. They like what these good men can provide for them. If they liked good men, they would pursue them when she is the peak of her sexual marketplace value.

There used to be a phrase "You can't turn a whore into a housewife, but apparently women and men have forgotten this.

The reality is that women HATE the good men. They will use the good men; they will pitch themselves out to be wife material to good men when they feel like their sexual marketplace value is beginning to decline. When a woman actually finds a good man who would cater to her and give her the attention that she thought she wanted, she discovers that she actually hates this man. But, this man is able to provide children and the traditional family that a BAD BOY wouldn't. He can make all of their college and consumer debt disappear. When a woman wants to settle down, they will prioritize safety and security above all other needs. They would love for the bad boys to fill this dual role, but they know that it's going to be a very long shot for that to happen.

Now, when they settle down with the good man, they find out that the good man is boring; he might not be as sexually aggressive or satisfying in bed. He's coming up short in delivering the pleasures and gratification that Chad or Tyrone did when she was doing late night double backflips on him.

Yes, the good man might be providing some good experiences; he's paying for all of the travel, and assuming all of the baby duties for the family. He's able to provide a nice house or living arrangements, a car or SUV for the wife, a spending account, and acceptance of her feminist ideology. He's the fool that believes in the nauseating phrase "Happy Wife, Happy Life."

Deep inside she may like the good man, but she doesn't LOVE the good man. She actually despises him for what he is in her life because her loins get moist for Chad and Tyrone.

This is why you women insist on going to "girl's nights out" and "girl's trips," places where she can play those flirty games that she's used to with all of the bad boys in Las Vegas and even in her hometown. She will rejoin the cougar fray right after the kids are produced and the house has been provided. She misses her old life, and this is because we live in a whore-ish culture where women think they can sleep around like men with no mental or psychological consequence. But, she has to settle down with the good man because he is willing to be a provider of the things that she's not able to, or willing to provide for herself. She HAS to deal with him if she wants safety and security.

The problem is that while she's out there fucking every Chad and Tyrone, the good man is out here bringing her flowers, writing poems, pulling out her chair and opening her car door as if she is the virtuous woman that she isn't. Meanwhile, she's been run through more times than the Holland Tunnel.

Time Thieves

"Women will rape you for your time." – Patrice O'Neal

Men, time is one of your biggest assets. It is one of the biggest things that you can give to a woman that you can never get back. You can always get your commitment back. You can always make back the money that you lost in pursuing or maintaining a relationship. But time, if given away at a certain period in your life, can never be recouped and returned at the same energy level that you were at when you gave that time away.

If you're a man in your 20's, you have time on your side but far too often these men give away their time frivolously in pursuit of women and relationships or trying to get laid, and they believe that this is going to be a good investment of that time, both short term, and long term. Now, if neither of these situations work, or your long term relationship or marriage ends in divorce, you will lose all of that time. You cannot get that time back. Any opportunities that you have in the future, you don't have the luxury of time to build yourself up.

That's why I encourage men to be careful before they give away their commitment and time. You will never be able to reproduce either; neither will you get another shot at it.

In terms of women specifically, they love to take your time away from other things that you enjoy, or other things that are going to make you better. She will never understand or accept that there are things that are more important than her in your life. She believes that she is the most important thing in your life and will demand that your attention or the time that SHE determines is free, is entitled to her. I have coached many men that have taken time away from many things that would have made them better persons, financially and otherwise, in order to placate or please the women in their lives. Many times, the things that they did in exchange didn't benefit anyone, not even the woman. It was just considered quality time. Most times, it came at a financial cost: Trips to the farmer's markets, meaningless hours at the festival or county fair, binge-watching episodes together, or brunch dates with her gal pals. All of these things resulted in you absorbing your emotions, and getting yourself distracted from your ultimate purpose. This is the time that you cannot get back.

If you are going home every day to someone whom you have given your commitment to, but you are not where you want to be, yet you are giving three-four hours a night to her, then she is stealing your time, and she has no problem doing it. The most important thing that she needs from you is your attention. In fact, take away time from a woman, and watch her interest decrease; she will hop back on the cock carousel and find someone else's time to monopolize.

For the married men who are reading this, you have no other choice. You've boxed yourself in. That's why I am the voice for younger men to let them know what they are getting into before they are sold the pipe dream of "LOVE." If you want to make something out of your life, avoid marriage and long-term commitment, until you have fulfilled your purpose.

In the 40+ years that I have lived, I have yet to hear a man tell me that he has seen a positive return in the time that he have invested in women. Learn the law of diminishing returns and apply it to women, and you will win at life. Trust me; women will always be there. Find things that are more valuable to you and that will ADD to your life. Everything a woman brings to you will produce a debt in time and a dent in your resources. Every single muthafuckin' thing!

Value the time that you have when you're young. You have all of the advantages. You are young, you are energetic, and you are smart. You will not be that for very long, and this is your window to take advantage of these strengths. If you waste your precious hours listening to women drone on about the inconsequential activities that they experienced in their day, the silly text exchanges with their bestie, the relentless re-caps of the mind numbing reality TV shows that she watches, you will be in a far worse position in your life than if you had been applying your passion, drive, and energy to something that could help you advance your life.

These things always take priority over women. If you pursue them and achieve your goals and dreams, the line of women that are willing to comply with your lifestyle will be endless.

Ditch Dating & Dating Apps

I have met some really cool women online. Women who were looking for friendship, relationships, one-night stands, friends with benefits and even marriage. I've enjoyed many of them in each one of these aspects. Unfortunately, their expectations have gotten more ridiculous the more time that I spent with them.

Things to Consider Regarding Dating Apps

- People spend on average, eight hours per week on dating apps. Add in the time that it takes setting up dates offline, meeting for dates, prepping, etc., and it becomes an incredible time wasting activity. The constant Ping-Pong texting is a distraction during the day, a distraction while driving and a distraction from productive activities. Women will text you back and forth like it's a serve-volley tennis match, soaking up the attention that you are giving her, while you can't even focus on the things that you need to do.

- The number of single mothers on dating sites is too damn high! Dating apps are a rest haven for single mothers. The vast majority of them will be bringing children to the party and it's something that you should avoid at all cost. Do not date single mothers!

- There are some unusually tall women at dating apps and they tend to hold strong to the six-foot or taller requirement, which is understandable. Taller women tend to be either fetishized or treated more masculine than their shorter counterparts, so I can imagine that they don't get approached in public as often, unless they are models. If you fall short of their requirement, then you have little chance because their ego can't handle being seen with a shorter male. Don't be offended; just avoid these egomaniacs. Log back in to the app in six months and most of them will still be there.

- The amount of women that have a few extra pounds is off the charts on dating apps. The average weight of women in the United States is 168lbs. That's the average! So, this is another fetishized group, commonly referred to as BBW's (Big, Beautiful Women). Men will show these women a lot of interest in private and even have sex with them, but refuse to be seen with them in public. This confuses the BBW's ego and leaves them believing that they can get someone to commit to them long term. The reality is that these women are massive liabilities for anything long term and even short term. Sometimes, it is hard to determine if the girl that you're looking at in photos is actually over-weight, so just consider anyone with only photos of the neck and above a BBW.

- Dating apps are a rest haven for feminists and women with unusual dating standards. These are the women who proudly exclaim that they "can't cook" or that "their career comes first." These women are very liberal and often brag about their college degrees and jobs. If you are a man with any pride, you would stay far away from feminists. They pose many dangers to your life and have more student debt that you can imagine. They are looking for their beta male provider to bail them out. The truth is that many of them have exceeded their expiration date.

- Be cautious of attention seekers. These women may live far away from you and express a high interest in meeting you. They have a high likelihood of flaking and ghosting on you since you are nowhere near them, so they have the security in knowing that they would never meet you in person to confront them if they ghost on you. You will spend way too much time and attention on them for the off chance that you would meet them. Let them pursue you, or move on.

Dating is a major time waster and online dates rarely yield positive returns, other than the occasional pump and dump. Think of the things that you can accomplish when you take that off the table and put your attention on the things that could help you. When I stopped doing those things, my life got exponentially better. When I took dating off the table, my life improved emotionally and financially and my businesses flourished. You CAN have it all men, just not at the same time. Ask yourself this: Is the time spent on online dating worth trading what you could actually become in this life.

When Things Don't Add Up, Start Subtracting

Full disclosure, I did not come up with this phrase, but I don't remember where I heard it. It may have been in the comment section of one of my videos or a comedian may have said it. I can't really remember. But, it definitely stuck with me and became useful in my engagements with women. The basic premise of it is that if you let one get close to you, watch for the red flags.

Many times things don't make sense when you are learning about someone. Instead of making it make sense, we continue to add things that don't make sense to try to make it make sense. Does that make sense?

This makes for a much larger problem. Instead of adding on to the problem, I may be able to take something from the problem and see if the situation actually works, or if it gets rid of the problem altogether. **So, when things don't add up, start subtracting.**

Sh*t Tests

Relationships with women come with a ton of sh*t tests. Women use shit tests to determine your true interest in her and value to her. These things are done subconsciously, and some, intentionally. They ALL do it! At all stages of the relationship. It reveals a lot regarding their insecurities and whether they trust your intentions. Sometimes, her girlfriends will coax her into shit testing you just to see your reaction and provide for fodder during their next girls night out. Or, she may be dating multiple men and put one or both into a series of shit tests, and the one who passes survives to stay with her. It's a dumb mating strategy, because she could lose all of her suitors, but there will always be more simps waiting to board her slave ship.

Example Of Sh*t Tests

1. Basic – Asking, "Do I look fat in the dress?"

2. Advanced – Showing up late for dates, asking to be rescued at the most inopportune times

3. Nuclear – Going to dinner with ex, girls nights out or trips to Vegas or Miami

Every man has experienced and recognized basic level sh*t tests. They can be used to get your attention or to receive some validation from you that they don't feel that they are getting. This can range from asking if they appear fat in an outfit or getting a haircut and not telling you to see if you'd notice. If you don't notice her three inch trim job, she overreacts with disappointment for not recognizing "major changes" in her appearance. A woman will lose it emotionally if these basic sh*t tests aren't handled properly and swiftly. Even your mother will use this shit test on you.

In the early part of a relationship, another example of a basic level shit test would be letting the dinner bill sit on the table for a long period of time without acknowledging it. Women will wait an entire hour with the bill sitting on the table and she won't even look in its direction. If she doesn't reach for it, she has no intentions of contributing to the date and is waiting for you to grab it. Grabbing it makes it yours, and ultimately nullifies her need to pay.

An advanced sh*t test involves not only trying to get your attention or getting you emotional; it will result in her attempting to steal your time. An example of this is asking you to come to her rescue at the most inopportune time. She may claim to have car trouble while you're at work or picking up your kids from school to see if you will drop your important commitments just for her. She wants to see if your inner Captain Save-A-Hoe will overtake your logical need to keep your job and take care of your main responsibilities. Have her find her AAA card and handle it like a big girl. She may also have other suitors in the hopper and using an advanced shit test will allow her to narrow down her list by seeing who runs to her cry for help. Oddly enough, the man who doesn't save her may be in the driver's seat, while the monkey-simp that runs to her rescue may come off as desperate. Women are weird that way. You make the wrong move; it could cost you the game.

A nuclear sh*t test is usually a cry for help or her trying to blow the relationship up, forcing your hand to dump her. If she is the dumpee (the person who got dumped), then she can play the victim. So, she might become unresponsive to your messages for a night to make you wonder where she is. Or she might reveal that she is meeting an ex-boyfriend for dinner or visiting him while he's in town. Or, the most overlooked nuclear test; insisting on going to girls night's out or girls trips. Once you get to this point of the relationship, it's just about over. But, she will put the control in your hands and if you fail this test, you are her monkey-simpanzee forever, and she will walk all over you while she's doing double backflips on Chad or Tyrone. If you pass the nuclear sh*t test, you now have an ex-girlfriend, but you also have a "victim" that will claim that you were an assh*le or even something worse.

These shit tests are downright manipulation and are emotionally abusive because they have taken a stable situation and intentionally made it unstable, and based on your reaction; she blames or credits you on how you handle it. It is the mad science of all mad scientists. These games, if played with the wrong man, can be very dangerous to women. And, many women embrace that "danger" element because of the excitement that it creates for her. Chad's and Tyrone's are often compliant with her shit testing.

If you can't handle the shit testing, then they attack your masculinity and say you're not strong enough to play the game. But, these games are nothing short of mental abuse to men and have nothing to do with your masculinity and more to do with your patience. Dealing with women shouldn't be a Navy Seal exercise.

When men deal with these shit tests, it can be downright confusing because they are being emotionally vulnerable and they are seeking understanding of why things are happening the way they are, but women aren't filling them in on the game. You're considered weak if you don't play their games.

What I've found is that instead of putting up with these abusive tactics and trying to impress women with my masculine frame, I simply subtract myself from these situations. I walk away and let them find another victim.

I had a girlfriend who would disappear during the 'hook-up hours' of the evening. This is the time of the evening when you get home from work, shower, get dressed, go on your date, come home, and fuck. Then by 10:30 or 11pm, you're done and ready for bed. Usually around 7pm, she would not respond to phone calls or text messages but would all of a sudden pop up around 10 or 10:30pm claiming that she was reading and making dinner.

Another would claim to have great relationships with all of her exes and would routinely go to dinner with them, without me of course.

Ultimately, a lot of things didn't add up and I would make more additions to try to make her make sense, but all that did was give her more fuel to continue to run circles around me. These behaviors would get an emotional response from me and she would feed off of the attention that I was giving her. Do you think a woman would stop the bullsh*t if you keep giving her more attention and adoration?

The best thing I did was to stop adding and trying to make sense of things, but rather start to SUBTRACT. Subtract myself from the situation. Once I subtracted myself from the situation, everything got better. The games immediately stopped and I regained control of the relationship or what remained of it.

Marriages go through this as well and usually by a wife that the man is probably not having sex with anymore, the classic sexless marriage that I talked about in chapter 1. If you see that you're continuing to dump more into the relationship to make it work, going to marriage counselors to understand her, reading books on how to re-ignite the spark and going to the church reverend to see what the bible says, then you may be fighting a futile battle. All of these additions to make up for the deficit in your marriage, it is time to start subtracting. Subtracting will get the bullshit in line really quick.

We have all been blue-pilled mangina monkey simpanzees and I have experienced many of the things that you, the reader, are probably experiencing today. You might be going through this right now and it may be the reason you picked up this book or decided to adopt this philosophy. I was in the same boat and there were men before me that helped me understand the things that didn't make sense.

Things didn't add up until I started subtracting. Remove yourself from ALL shit tests. Don't get emotional, don't argue, and don't fight. Just walk away. If she leaves, she leaves with a lesson. And, you will be better for it.

CHAPTER 6

PRIORITIZE YOUR LIFE

Some men believe that you're not a real man if you're not out chasing ass and pursuing women. There is a time and place for everything, but you're not on earth just to appease women. A little pleasure maybe, but if you don't think I'm cool or you think I'm lame because I'm spending the majority of my time focusing on myself and the things that I enjoy, then I'll just have to be a lame.

In this chapter, we're going to talk about a few things that you will have to do to navigate your way through life as a young man in order to get to the point when you're older, more mature, and wiser. These are some of the things that I would've told myself at 18 years old and stuck with them.

We've already talked about how important your time is to you and why you should value it. You have to make the things that matter in your life a priority. Ultimately it is about understanding how to prioritize the important things in your life so that the rest of your life will look fantastic.

Organizing time and learning how to make it work for you is a big deal. Some guys waste a lot of time because as a young person, you feel like you're going to be here forever. But, life goes by fast, especially as your responsibilities increase. While you're here, you need to be productive or you'll soon be living on the street.

Think about the amount of time that you spend on things that are not going to benefit you, or worse, things that impact you negatively. Most of the time, you're spending that time on women or with people who aren't going anywhere with their lives. You must watch out for yourself and remember that people don't value your life like you would hope they would.

I've always felt this about people who offer me drugs. You don't value your own life, so you do drugs when you're bored to entertain yourself. But, you also expect me to listen to you about how valuable my drug experience will be.

If you're spending that amount of time with people who are not going to bring an exceptional amount of value to your life, then you're wasting time. Men, you don't have time to waste!

Think about Tupac Shakur, the hip-hop superstar who died at the age of 25. Some of you guys might be too young to know about him. But, there are stories about the amount of time that he spent in the recording studio making albums. At the time of his death he had released just four albums including one that released while he was doing a prison stint. After his death he released eight more albums, most of them containing unreleased songs. He would spend time just laying down the vocals on rough tracks that had not been finalized by the producer. He didn't care about that, telling his producers that they could do the mixing and finalizing later when he's not in the studio, but while he was there, he wanted to be as productive as possible. He worked like he didn't know how much time he was going to be afforded in life. He didn't have time to be out at the club celebrating his life and indulging in the things that would slow down his progress. Well, at least not every day. And as we now know, he didn't have a lot of time left on earth. But, what he left after his death was enough music and movies to continue to inspire people 10-20 years later.

Prioritizing Your Money

Establishing the basics with regards to money must be prioritized. Learn about the banking and financial system and how it works. Open a bank account and manage it. Learn about what interest rates are and how they affect you. I was told as a teenager that there are two types of people: **Those who pay interest and those who earn interest**. You want to be the one who is earning more interest than you are paying. Know how money works and how you can make money work for you, instead of just trading time for money on your job. Even if you don't want to be a millionaire or if you just want to live a minimalist lifestyle, you still have to know these things so you can be a more astute and financially responsible individual. You will have more resources to choose from to provide the life that you want to live. The #freeagentlifestyle. Don't wait too long in learning these things and how these systems work.

Start off with these things and learn how to make them work for you:

- Dow Jones Index
- NASDAQ Index
- Ways to Invest and get a return
- What is crypto currency?

Here are some other things to consider:

- Learn that trading your time for money is not always in your best interest. It may be the very thing that is making you poor. If earning more money is what you want, then you must learn to look for talent-based jobs. Jobs that pay you to produce results instead of trading your time. Make your talent pay you.
- Learn what residual income is. Learn what passive income is.
- Determine if college/university is right for you and if you will need it. If you're going to college without a real plan or just to please

your parents, family and friends, then you are setting yourself up for financial failure. Why spend tens of thousands of dollars without a plan? Maybe explore a trade and other blue-collar fields that may give your more opportunities when you're younger. Maybe you can go to a liberal arts college and learn a trade and have something to fall back on during tough economic times.

- Blue-collar work and trades are making a comeback. There was a time, fifty years ago that most men worked in blue-collar fields. The world was more industrial and the jobs required muscle, hard physical work, and grit. These men worked at the plant or the factory and they were able to provide well for their families. They worked on cars, they worked as electricians, as carpenters, and they worked with their hands. With the advances in technology, many jobs have moved indoors to offices and imprisoning cubicles. These jobs are less demanding physically and require you to sit in your desk for long periods of time just as you did in school. But, something tells me that those types of jobs are ending for many. How many of these corporations have to collapse and ruin economies of entire cities for us to understand that these industries may be a house of cards? The days where going to college and loading yourself with $150,000 in student loans in hopes of getting a $45,000/year salary are disappearing. Women are taking over those jobs. They provide them with the safety and security to believe that this is a great career path, but to me, it's just a slow death.

- Explore certification; think about getting your CDL, and driving a truck. Research other types of certifications. These jobs give you flexibility and independence. They are also in high demand and often times will lead you into becoming a business owner. These jobs are often the last to get eliminated in a tough economy. If you know how to work with your hands and have a skill, you will always be in demand.

Register a Business

You should already have a business registered for yourself. Even if it's a side hustle. When you have it registered, and a business banking account is established, you'll be more likely to work on that business when you have free time. I had my first business registered by the age of 18. Even if you're in your fifties, do it now. It's never too late.

Take Care of Your Health

This is a high priority and one of your major responsibilities. Take your health seriously. You only get one body and you will never get a chance to trade it in if it fails. You're last name isn't Kardashian. You don't get to trade in body parts when you're not satisfied with them.

Don't believe that you have to look like a fitness competitor like you see on Instagram or resemble a Marvel superhero, but you should be functional. You're joints shouldn't be creaking. You shouldn't be significantly overweight. You MUST take care of your body. If you maintain your health, true wealth will follow. Wealth without good health is pointless. You will be able to work longer and harder, you'll have energy to go out and make money, and you'll have time to get out and do things to recreate yourself.

Take care of your mental health, your physical health, and your sexual health. Get a clean bill of health from your physician.

This Is What Happens When You Prioritize Women

Think about this and let this sink in. Men spend too much time thinking about women who aren't even giving them a second thought. You see a woman in a coffee shop that is visually pleasing. Her presence, her attire, her smell, the way she walks, and how her hair bounces after each carefully placed step is stuck with you all day, and maybe even into the next day if you didn't beat your meat to her that night. If you didn't talk to her, you've thought about what you should have said or how you should've bucked up and got her name at least, or better yet, how you should have got her number.

You want to know the painful truth? That same woman didn't even give you a second thought. You didn't even register in her distracted mind; much less make an impression on her. She hasn't even considered you a possibility but you have completely lost focus from the things that matter because of this one woman. Focus men!

Women cannot be a priority in your life because they will always do what is in their best interest. They see you merely as a utility if you involve yourself with one. Understand that! They are never going to put you first. Once you've provided everything they believe they can get from you, they will not hesitate to bump you off and swing to a new branch.

If you are the type of person to look for the best in women, and if you're foolish enough to marry a women and think that they won't divorce rape you, then you have great faith. If you're willing to roll the dice and take that gamble then consider this. If you prioritize your life, you will attract some of the better quality women in terms of looks than you will ever imagine is possible.

But, always remember, no matter how they look, the results will be the same. They still have the same nature and they are backed by the state to withdraw everything that you have worked so hard for through your rectum, via the family court. They believe that with the simple act of marriage, that they are entitled to this.

Men are spending too much time in their day thinking about what to say to women, how to pursue them, when to respond to their text messages, and what to say when they see one. Time that you should be spending as a man living the #freeagentlifestyle, time that should be focused on being productive. A by-product of that drive is that you could earn more money, you'll have more opportunities in business and life, you'll have more options, you'll be able to focus better, and you'll be able to provide yourself with more time and opportunities to travel. You will get more when you focus on THAT! Those are the gifts that will keep on giving.

Once you have more money, you will obtain more power and opportunities. Once you have more opportunities, you will have a chance to make more money.

The gift that doesn't keep on giving is prioritizing women. For men, the end game with women is sex. We want to have sex with them, PERIOD. Some monkey simpanzee might read this and want to tell you that they want to enjoy all of the intelligent conversations, companionship and heavy petting without the sex. These men may just be saying what they believe women want to hear. They certainly aren't being sincere or authentic.

The honest men know that sex is the ultimate biological imperative. The better part of a sexual experience (the most important part for men) will take an average of about 15-45 minutes. The rest of the time that you spend with women is to get to the sexual aspect of the relationship.

Men will spend five-six hours easily, just trying to get in bed with women. THAT is where you are wasting your time, men. Understand that this is not a waste of time for women. Usually, they are getting something from it. They are getting fed, free validation, a listening ear, non-sexual attention, entertainment, and drinks. They have no problem monopolizing your time, and the more time you surrender, the better it turns out for her. They don't believe that you are entitled to receive ANYTHING in return for the time and attention that you are freely giving them. The fact that they were born as females entitles them to everything above.

This is where men make critical mistakes, because they lose focus on the gift that they keep on giving. You could be a millionaire by the age of 40 if you do not prioritize women. You could be a millionaire! It seems impossible and ridiculous for me to write that, but just think about the amount of time and money that you have wasted by going out to dates, going to nightclubs, spending time on dating apps and texting women.

When I Prioritized Women

I have prioritized women in my life trying to get the P-sleeve. What I've learned is that it is a waste of time and ultimately, I realized that you cannot pay enough attention to a woman. You cannot win! At some point, they are going to want more, and they'll view you as a bottomless pit of attention to give her freely. It's a thirst that cannot be quenched. In any marriage or relationship, they want more quality time and attention to be provided by you. You cannot satisfy women, you cannot make them happy. If you start off with giving her a lot of attention, then suddenly pull back because you have to do other real life responsibilities, she will pull back from you.

So, why prioritize all of that time and energy on them?

When you prioritize a woman, you end up getting less quality women and you eliminate the chance of you becoming a millionaire. A millionaire in terms of dollars, business opportunities, opportunities in life, establishing strong brotherhood relationships and friendships that can help you in life and business. This is where you should be spending the majority of your time.

As the saying goes, you will lose money chasing women, but you will never lose women chasing money. When this happens, the quality of women will be much better than the women you're spending time giving puppy love attention to. Women will always be there. Opportunities may not.

For my 18-25 year old Free Agents who may be struggling to meet women and you're looking for ways to improve your chances with women, I'm going to tell you one thing, this is the one thing that I would tell my 18-year-old self. When you turn 35-45 years old and you have prioritized yourself, you will not be able to beat the women away. You will have more opportunities with better quality women than you will ever had in your life and you will have the best sex in your life.

At my age, having been through marriage and owning my own businesses, I have access to women from the age of 21-51 and I have enough options to choose from. The best part of it is that it's easier than it was when I was doing the pursuing. I don't have to do very much to get sex. I don't feel any pressure returning text messages or trying to keep their attention because there is always another woman making herself available to me based on the lifestyle that I live. But, I would rather use my free time to focus on the things that matter.

CHAPTER

7

THE IMPORTANCE OF SELF CARE

A lot of times we get bogged down when we pursue relationships and the pursuit of wealth and happiness; we think that women should be the center of our universe. A lot of times we're putting out so much effort and energy towards being a provider that we lose sight of what's truly important. We're not here just to provide for ourselves and other people, we are here to make sure that we have the best possible life and have fun. Lest you forget, this is your one life and I want to make sure that you use this one life properly.

These are the things that you need to consider when it comes to the importance of self-care for men. You do not have to do all of them; you don't even have to do most of them. But, these things should be considered as a matter of your physical health, your mental health and your overall well-being.

When we talk about taking care of one's self, a lot of times, women do a better job, for two reasons. Mainly, because of society's expectations to always put their best foot forward, appearance-wise. The other reason is that they do a better job of prioritizing therapeutic modalities to assist them with their physical and mental recovery. Lord knows where we would be if they didn't get the help that they needed!

But, we must do the same things for ourselves, gents. We can't walk around being sloppy and slovenly just because we are not pursuing long-term relationship and marriage. We have to care about ourselves, and we have to do our best to keep ourselves healthy, hygienic, and clean. We must make sure that we are physically and emotionally strong.

Now, these are a couple of things that I suggest that you consider when you are emphasizing self-care.

Getting Massages

No, I'm not talking about the happy ending massages that have been the focus of police dragnets, snares, and traps recently. However, if you want to incorporate those in your life legally, I certainly do not pass judgment on you.

The massages that I am referring to are the therapeutic massages, sports massages, and Swedish massages that you can get in a spa setting. Executives and wealthy men already partake because they understand the importance of it. But, you can be the average man and with the right budgeting you can find an affordable massage.

I used to train a massage therapist for two years and we made an agreement since our rates were similar that we could exchange our services equally. I would train her twice a week and she would give me massages twice a week. I would go to her place and lay on the table and let her do that work.

I wouldn't suggest that you get that many massages. Although they felt good, it was bit of an overkill in terms of my schedule. I would suggest that you get a massage once every two weeks or once a month, to release the toxins and stress from your muscles so you can perform.

Grooming & Hair Cuts

Keep up your grooming mainly to feel better about yourself. Some men understand the power behind simple grooming, and there are some funny videos on YouTube on how men feel before and after a visit to the barber.

I'm not telling you how to style your hair; I'm only saying that you should make a conscious effort to keep it trimmed, clean, and healthy for pride alone.

I know it's funny to hear someone who is bald talking about keeping your hair in order, but I do have a full beard that requires maintenance and I do my best to keep this shaggy, mountain man beard in order. I also go to shops that groom it to make sure it is maintained and even.

When you go to a barbershop, you experience a sense of brotherhood that you cannot get in today's world. Women want to invade male spaces everywhere and with the rare exception of the single mother who brings her child in the shop, the space is generally 100% male, and men are free to talk about subject matters that women can't handle or that women don't need to know. No butt hurt feelings, and men can share things with younger men that can make their lives better.

So keep your hair straight, clean, and groomed. The next thing I'm going to suggest is much more controversial for men.

Getting Manicures and Pedicures

Getting manicures and pedicures are often viewed as feminine. The same can be said about cooking. We make jokes about women and cooking, and even go as far as assigning this as a woman's duty to her family; alas the June Cleaver model. However, the professional culinary world is one that is dominated by men. So, it goes without saying; if men can cook, they can get manicures and pedicures.

Keeping your nails clean is not a female things and it will help you immensely, especially if you are a sales person, entrepreneur, or businessman. Similar to cleaning your teeth in the morning, you should keep your nails clean, trimmed and healthy. Let's get rid of those yellow toenails too. Hygiene is a major part of the Free Agent Lifestyle

Your hands, like your face, are one of the first things that people see. If they see your hands, face, and hair being unkempt, then you'd be an object of negative judgement when trying to conduct business. As far as it being a feminine activity, just don't get the clear finger nail polish at the end, make sure that they buff your nails, NO CLEAR POLISH men! And, don't even think about getting any other color nail polish, unless you're in a heavy metal rock band.

This is not just for white-collar workers. I know many blue-collar workers that keep their appearance presentable and it helps them with their business.

Focusing on these things will give you something to do with the time you'll have on your hands living the Free Agent Lifestyle. It's about prioritizing yourself and keeping yourself busy, and your mind off of the P-Sleeve all day.

Eating the Right Food

Take care of your body and stop ingesting poisons. These food companies don't care about you and a lot of people think; "These companies wouldn't poison us to make a profit. They wouldn't give us processed foods or chemicals that might give us cancer. Would they?" YES THEY WOULD! These companies will feed you anything as long as it turns in a buck for them. Even if it contributes to your death and demise, they will market to your children to cover their lost consumer. If you're going to continue to eat poison, they're going to continue to feed it to you.

Cheap Food

When I was in college, I remember certain fast food restaurants used to be known for their inexpensive menu. Some have so-called Dollar menu items where you can literally get fed for less than $3 dollars. Now, if you think about it, you're saving money, but at the same time, you're shaving days and weeks off your life for a few dollars and a little convenience.

I'm always cautious of where I purchase my meat and where I get my dry snacks. Most of the time, they are from different markets because I don't trust everyone's food. Some items aren't good for you long term and you shouldn't be consuming them. You have to know where your food is coming from. You have to know what you're placing into your body. Learn to read food labels. If it's making your body look oddly shaped and fat is being stored in your body in places where fat doesn't belong, consider devising a new nutrition plan.

If you look at the people who consume junk and fast food over a long period of time, you'd discover that they have fat stored in them in places where fat doesn't belong. People have fat along the side of their hips and triple fat roll flaps around their stomach and this is not natural. How in the hell is your body morphing into that? The reason why is because they are consuming products that their body doesn't know what to do with all the unhealthy food that they are eating in excess.

Make sure you're eating clean foods. Make sure you're eating balanced meals with greens and fresh veggies. Try to avoid restrictive diets that can only deliver temporary results. Make sure you are eating meals that are spaced out during the day rather than gorging on heavy meals every 4-5 hours. Eating at the right time of the day is critical. Overeating at night is dangerous. We need to change our eating habit, brothers.

Remember, when you change your lifestyle, it will not come together all at once. It takes time and you should be patient enough to start habit changing so you can look back two-three years from now and see how far you came. **You can change your fucking life in one year!**

This is important men! I want you guys to live to 80, 85, and 90 and in perfect health, with your strength unabated. Select proper foods. Don't get your foods because they are cheap, because cheap foods are ones that are going to kill you.

Working Out

The big thing that I want you to know in this chapter is that working out consists of a consistent program that you will participate in for the remainder of your life. It is a regimen. I am not telling you to try to look like He-Man because that's not for everyone.

Make sure you keep your body moving. Your body was designed to be a machine, not sitting behind a desk for 8-10 hours a day, and commuting to work for 2-3 hours before and after your butt hits the chair. Our vessels were not designed to be sedentary; they were designed to be moving and working, and your food is the power source to fuel your machine.

Moving is how we evolved to our bi-pedal position from crawling on all fours. I have a fear that someday we will just evolve into being seated animals, where we would need a chair everywhere we went or we couldn't function. Sadly, some of us are already like this.

Make sure you are conducting a workout program, any program. I'm not here to tell you what program works for you. That is what you are going to discover. We are fortunate enough to live in a time where gyms are on every corner now, replacing fast food joints, but far behind the daily coffee shops. Working out has become the "IT" thing to do, so finding a program that fits your needs and skill level should not be difficult. Experiment with what works for you. For me, big box gyms just won't do. There are too many posers and gym thots in there trying to distract everyone and feel important. I feel more comfortable in a small gym setting and even better, working out from home. I bought equipment that I like, and can usually get in 35-50 minutes of working out before I leave my house.

Not having enough time is not an excuse that Free Agents will be using so let's get after it! Get your workout done, get your body moving, and your body will take care of you. You want to be that old guy at age 52 moving well, not the 52 year old that is taking twenty-two versions of medications just to keep your ass alive, just making you a pharmaceutical simp. You don't want to be that person. You want to be the person that is fueling your body to make sure that it performs over the long term. You want to be here for a long time. You want to be functional by that particular point.

Keep A Fresh, Simple and Clear Appearance

Put on your good clothes! But, keep it simple. You're not trying to make yourself a target for women who are looking to cash in on some of your resources. I'm not telling you to go out there and be super fly and spend money on an expensive wardrobe. For the most part, we are doing our best to be incognito. Make every attempt you can to not draw attention to yourself. With that being said, here are a few things that Free Agents need to consider when they are focusing on keeping their appearance in order.

Make sure you buy clothes that fit properly and that look good, for you. Again, we are not trying to stand out, but we are trying to be comfortable. Wearing the latest styles could be considered standing out. For instance, if you have ripped expensive tight fitting jeans or overly baggy jeans that you are sagging way below your belt line, then you will stand out and be judged.

I tend to wear basic clothes, like my favorite Old Navy $10 V-neck black t-shirt when I'm not wearing Coach Gang Wear. It is a soft shirt and the sleeves are cut so they don't run too long down my arms, to make them look ill fitting. These shirts fit so well that I ordered eight of the same shirts and I can wear them throughout the week and not put too much thought into what I'm wearing and what I need to match with.

Solid colors, that fit well are preferred with limited-to-no logos on them that could make the shirt look unbalanced. This allows me to feel better about what I'm wearing. Your clothes don't have to cost a lot of money.

Take Long Drives

Some of my best ideas have come from taking long drives down the highway or when I was taking road trips and learning the lay of the land. I use a recorder to save and transcribe my ideas later if I am not able to write them down. If I don't record or write them, then I forget them. Many of my best ideas are lying on the interstates across the United States because I said to myself, "I'll remember that," only to forget them by the end of the night.

Taking road trips helps clear my head, and the open space and sounds of the highway stimulate thought, similar to long showers at home. There is not much else to do when you're strapped to a seat and coasting down the highway. But, there is something to be said when you're sitting between four walls and a roof. A lot of good ideas seem to be trapped on the outside of the walls, and you're fighting your limited thoughts on the inside.

Get out and hit the open road. Enjoy, and explore some of the beautiful locations in your country.

CHAPTER 8

YOU ARE THE PRIZE

Men, You Are The Prize! This is a difficult concept for most men to handle. When men hear this, they interpret this as me telling them to give up their pursuit of P-sleeve and ass, but they are missing the big picture.

What I am telling them is that the pursuit of their goals takes priority over everything else, to stop providing and supporting women and to be willing to go solo with almost everything that they do. There is a lot of social programming that I'm trying to reverse, but some men who can't see any other option but to put women on a pedestal naturally react negatively to this philosophy. They start by calling me names, attacking my masculinity, or downright shaming me to get me back in compliance. I get it, trust me, I get it. But, if you thought the first seven chapters were a hard red pill to swallow, then this chapter will be an even thicker, rougher pill.

It's hard to get a man's brain to grip this concept. It's hard to understand after all of the conditioning that has been done with books, magazines, music, and movies that we're supposed to think differently. These forms of media have conditioned us with beautiful lyrics and imagery to be blue pilled simps. The lessons of falling in love and living happily ever after are present everywhere we look, and with every ear that is open. But, the story of maintaining relationships and working through problems is missing and women believe that if there are problems then it's time to give up. There are no major bumps and hard times depicted in movies, just perfection. The courts make it easy for women to just give up and collect cash and prizes through no-fault divorces, without any real reason other than "I'm not happy." Just blow it up, take what's his, keep what's hers and start over.

We've been taught that women are the prize. That we are supposed to pursue them, go after them and cater to their needs. That we are supposed to court them, wait on them, and shower them with gifts to show how much we want them.

We're supposed to bring them in, support them, and make them happy and to complete them. We're also supposed to provide entertainment for them and validate them every opportunity we have. In return, she might give you some physical contacts, some P-Sleeve.

Women have used this psychology to their advantage, to collect dates, free drinks and meals, jewelry, clothes, vacations, services (moving furniture), free rent, homes, and cars. Whatever you can imagine. They feel that men should provide these things and more in exchange for their time...and nothing more. If she wants to give you more, she can choose to. If she wants to give you nothing, then a man should just be satisfied with her company.

Our desire to sleep with women has led us to believe that they deserve to receive all of these things using the chance of sex as a lure. But, I've always believed that sex is an equal exchange, meaning that they received just as much pleasure during the act as I did. The older and better that I got in bed; she actually received more pleasure than I did. To top that, you must realize that men are doing 90% of the work in bed. Most of the time, she is just lying there. The act requires her to submit and be taken control of, so sex amounts to her just giving in and being under the man's control.

Putting Women on a Pedestal

In every form of media, the female form is idolized. Don't get me wrong, women are physically beautiful. Well, many of them are, and it's easy to be distracted by what they put out into the world for all of us to gaze at, all while calling us perverts for doing exactly what they expect, and quite frankly want us to do, and that is giving them attention! They need it. They crave it. Another example of women's lack of agency when it comes to taking responsibility for the decisions.

Other than their physical gifts, the majority of them fall short in terms of providing anything more. This is where men get confused. After a trip to the body shop, they become a massive liability and much like a house, you begin to work more to keep her than she is giving back. Your attachment to her emotionally is why you continue to work so hard for her, but in reality, she is setting fire to your money and your time.

Men are actually the assets to 97% of all relationships. We are the providers of safety, security, and protection. We have the physical strength and athleticism to do the dirty and dangerous work, make repairs, hunt for food, and take the risks. We are the financial sustainers that allow many families to exist intact today. Of course, there are exceptions to this rule, but there aren't many.

For far too long, society has taken advantage of men's weakness for women's physical form, and placed the female as the object of desire. What we fail to realize is that it is men who are the success objects, because without the things that men provide, societies would not exist. Period! So, who should be placed on a pedestal?

We need to put our hopes, our dreams, and our desire to improve ourselves for our goals, our aspirations, and our priorities on a pedestal. Most men who do this find that they have women chasing them, rather than the other way around.

What men provide is measurable. What she provides is not.

Think about some of the things that I mentioned above that we could offer to women. Now, include these things:

- Homes
- Vehicles
- Income
- Financial Stability
- Paying off Loans/Debt
- Vacations/Trips
- Children
- Children's Education and care
- Retirement Plans

If you come up short in any of these things, she will let you know about it. She will push you to provide her with more, and if you can't provide her with more, the things that she offers you will slowly decrease and she will begin to market herself to others suitors, a.k.a monkey branching.

Women use this tactic to get homes purchased for them, cars, vacations, purses and other tangibles. If they see other people they know getting these things; they will press you to provide her with more. Her attitude and demeanor will change, like a spoiled child who doesn't get his way. She will lose respect for you and she will start placing herself in situations where there are other men to market to. This could be a new job, taking classes at the community college, girls' trips or girls' nights out.

I was dating a girl whose best friend was able to have her student loans paid off by her newlywed husband. At that point, that became a standard by which she would measure me or other men she dated. She believed that she was entitled to this and she expected it. It was also my cue to exit the relationship and save myself from making a horrible decision.

Now, here's a list of things that she can offer you.

- Love
- Loyalty
- Trust
- Respect
- Sexual attention & gratification

If you notice, none of these things are measurable. They are all subjective, based on her ego, and they can be removed and given to someone else based on her emotional state. They are all things that she can claim that she gives you, even if you feel that she doesn't. Since you can't measure them, she can deny that she's falling short.

Now, let's flip the scenario and say that you (husband/ boyfriend) find out that your neighbor's wife greets him at the door naked, ready to blow him and relieve the stress from a long day pounding the pavement. Or maybe, you hear that his wife is doing monkey double back flips on him three-four times a night and six times on weekends. If you let your wife or girlfriend know about her shortcomings and press her to step up her performance, what kind of response will you get from her? I'll let you play that scenario out in your head.

After all, she has a monopoly on your access to the P-sleeve. Aren't you able to request more attention and effort? Her response can be summed up with this attitude: "I don't have to give you anything! You're not entitled to my body. You have to earn it."

And, THIS is exactly what men should say when their wife or girlfriend starts complaining about not getting shit that their friends are posting all over social media. "You're going to have to earn it!"

In today's dating and relationship climate, men offer far more to women than what women are capable of providing to men. We provide more value and tangible goods and services. That's why when you try to remove them from your home or divorce them; they fight you tooth and nail. They take you to court and use the legal system to keep some or all of the benefits that you have provided them with. You never see men trying to recover anything that women have provided in a relationship, because there wasn't much to begin with.

Women are always trying to get far more value out of men than they are actually worth. This is because we treat them as if they are the prize. They take up as much time as they can from you in order to satisfy their own need for attention. In the process, she takes away the things that you enjoy: opportunities for socializing outside of her presence, and any chance to earn more or hustle on the side to get more. At the same time, she wants you to provide more.

It's a lose-lose situation. You can't win, because if you don't give her attention, she'll look for it elsewhere. If you can't provide her with tangible items, she's look for someone else to provide them for her. Stop putting yourself in these games, men. You can't win!

Who Is Treated Like The Prize In Divorce Court?

One needs to look no further than family court to determine who the prize in nearly all relationships is. When partnerships implode, women lead the charge to the state's courthouses to get "what's fair" in the end. Women file for divorce more than 80% of the time and this is usually because she believes that she has an advantage in getting favorable rulings and cash and prizes. Men are less likely to file for divorce or seek equalization through the courts because there is not much to receive from her and way more to lose.

If you ever wanted to know who the prize in your relationship was, it is usually the one being dragged through the courts to get squeezed to provide alimony and child support and access to other government welfare.

Men, you are the fucking PRIZE!

Change the game

- Stop giving free validation to women. This empowers her and maintains her belief that she is the prize.

- No noticeable rubber necking when women walk near or past you. They have amazing peripheral vision and she is taking note of every head that she turns. Look straight ahead and keep you head high. Once you stop doing this, watch your world change.

- No free compliments. This is hard for a simp to do! They always have to tell women how beautiful she is, but they rarely get anything in return. Make her work for compliments. She doesn't get to just show up and receive instant validation for doing absolutely nothing. That just reinforces the idea that she is the prize.

- Stop playing the approach game. This is when you see pretty women in a public setting and feel the need to step up to her and get her number or ask if she's available. All this for doing nothing but breathing oxygen through her nose and expelling carbon dioxide through her mouth. Stop rewarding her for doing absolutely nothing for you.

- Stop providing free validation to women simply because they posted a photo online.

Women need to be working to get your attention. Believe me; women know a good thing when it's around. Well, most of the time. It's their 6th sense. Giving them that attention is the reason they behave the way they do.

The Prize on Social Media

Stop liking women's selfies on social media. She will post multiple versions of the same picture every day and get many men clicking like and commenting, telling her how beautiful she is. She needs this attention like a fish needs water. So she sets this trap that many monkey simpanzees fall for, believing that if they like her photos enough, they will get her attention. Never date a woman who does this sh*t. This is her way of keeping herself on the market and building her line of beta male orbiters.

There was a time where men and women would post selfies on social media sites. All of a sudden, it became a taboo for men to post them, as women would claim that it wasn't a manly thing to do. Oddly enough, she wouldn't hesitate to click the like button on The Rock's or Kevin Hart's selfie. But, your selfie game was just too much competition for her's AND was getting other women to give you the free validation that she was not able to keep up with. So, we started to see women complain about men posting selfies. Of course, men stopped posting them because men love to comply with women to seek an award from her and thus, her lane was clear. The attention seeking game was all hers.

Then it was; "stop posting photos with your shirt off, stop positing pictures next to fancy cars, stop posting pictures with guns, stop posting pictures of you having fun and traveling." All of this competes with her and makes you more attractive and desirable to others. Men were left posting memes and landscape pictures, making them less desirable, giving them less attention, and keeping the woman as the prize.

You Are the Prize, Act Like It

Men, you bring far more to a relationship than women can bring to the table. And that is before, during, and after the relationship starts and ends. Women are liabilities. Everything that they produce is a liability or something that comes to you at a cost. These costs are expected to be paid by you in order to receive their company and the immeasurable things that they provide.

Remember, you are the prize. Act like it

CHAPTER 9

F*CK BITCHES, GET MONEY

IT'S TIME TO GET YOUR MONEY RIGHT

These are the things that your father should have told you. If your father wasn't a monkey simpanzee, then you are already ahead of the game. If your father wasn't around or he was afraid to prepare for a world that was set up to make you fail, then you need to take notes.

Some of you guys have been trying to get your money right, but in the interim, you've been spending money on things, trying to impress others who don't give a damn about you. Or, maybe you take pride in being a provider to women, their children, and/or their families, and you don't realize that they are parasites and are leaching off of you. These people are all too ready to use you as a utility, but they really don't care about you.

Let me give you guys some key points based on how I was able to get my money right, despite all of the crazy things that happened in my life: the cross country moves, the job changes, the divorce raping, the child support issues, and overcoming the inner city hive mind mentality. I've been able to navigate my way back to get to a financial standing where I'm somewhat comfortable. Be ready to get yourself in a better financial position, by learning and following these key concepts.

Now, remember guys, I am not a financial planner or a financial advisor, so I am not giving you financial advice. I am simply offering you my experience on how to navigate your way into correcting your financial situation if you are in a tough bind. Also, if you're in a situation where you're not disciplined with your money or you're focusing on the wrong things, like entertaining women or focusing on buying more things to attract women, these key concepts will get you back on track.

Stop Paying To Access Women

This is the easiest things to do to change your financial picture. Stop paying to access women or to treat women. Specifically, dating!

The first problem with spending money to date is that you're meeting an individual who you don't know. Why the hell are you spending ANY money on them? Just think about this guys. Think about the brotherhood that you have and think about the brothers than you know. Do you actually spend money on them? How many rounds of drinks do you spend on your brothers? And, if you went out with your brothers, would you buy their entire meal?

If your answer is "No," or "Not that often," then there is no point in doing that for a stranger, somebody you barely know, simply because she has a clam between her legs. We've been conditioned to believe that it is our pleasure to pay for the time of women. Did you forget that you are the prize? So don't pay for dates when your financial picture is so cloudy.

If a women is not willing to date you because you are not offering to pay or not interested in going Dutch, a.k.a splitting the bill, then she is not the right person for you at this time of your life. If they are not satisfied with this arrangement, cancel them! They are not worth fucking up your finances. Create a plan and stick to your guns. No paying for dates.

The same rule applies to going to bars or nightclubs with the sole purpose of meeting women or scoping them out. And this definitely applies to going to strip clubs. Strip clubs are a rest haven for monkey simpanzees. You're just setting fire to your money; I don't care how much money you have or how much you make in a year. You're doing this to access women and a lot of times, you'll spend a helluva a lot more money than is necessary to access strippers. You're spending way too much hard earned money that you've traded time, and real blood, sweat, and tears for. So, try to focus on not spending that hard earned money to access women.

Avoid Buying (Financing) New Cars

Financing a vehicle is one of the worst financial decisions you will ever make. Of course, marriage is the absolute worst. The only exception is if you're spending cash for this purchase and/or using an auto broker to assist you with the purchase.

Even if you bought the car in cash, if you bought it new, the car is going to depreciate or lose its value by 7% before you drive it off the parking lot. By purchasing new vehicles, odds are that you've already over spent and if you financed the vehicle, you're already underwater on the bank loan.

I sold cars for about two months and I learned a lifetime worth of lessons in the short time working the lot.

Many auto buyers come in with very unreal expectations and basic math will be able to let them know whether they are in the Ball Park and standing outside with a ticket.

Most people are scared of car salesmen. The stereotype is that they are trying everything they can to screw you over. Honestly, a good car salesman is trying to make the deal work with you, your preferred terms, your ability to pay, and their general manager (GM). The GM is trying to work his magic with the banks and finance companies to get you the best deal relative to your available cash, negotiate price, and your credit score. Truth be told, the lots don't have a lot of wiggle room with the price on new vehicles and many car lots make their biggest money on used vehicles. Cue, the sleazy used car salesman wears a three-piece suit.

Many times, the salesmen and the GM may get you the best deal possible or even lose some gross, but if you're focused on the payment, you may end up financing a car for 5, 6, 7, or 8 years! Which is an insane term for a car payment.

While fearing the salesman and the GM is a legit concern, the finance department in the basement of the dealership is where the true damage is done. This is where you're buying mats, extended warranties, gap insurance, alarms and audio systems which will all ADD to the price that you have already negotiated upstairs with the salesmen. As a result, the monthly payment is going to increase and you are going to feel some type of way about it, like you're being screwed. That payment will bust your budget and to top it off, you've financed car mats for eight freaking years. Ouch! This area is where you get screwed and is the reason why you're underwater on the vehicle. Soon as your drive it off the lot, not only does the car depreciate in value but you owe way more than it's worth because of the length of the payment term and because you're paying interest on additional items that you don't need for the same payment term.

Don't buy new vehicles! Even if it is in cash, it is a bad investment. As a matter of fact, it's not an investment at all. It's just throwing away your money. Sure, you'll feel good driving your whip down the boulevard for a few months. But, making car payments will get old, especially when the vehicle is not as new and that new car smell has worn off, but you have five more painful years of new car payments.

If you need to purchase a vehicle, buy them used. I've bought several used vehicles in my life with cash and I've bought them at below blue book value with the use of an independent auto broker who knows how to look for deals and how to negotiate with general managers. All of these vehicles have treated me well and lasted three-five years, which is great for what I paid for them.

Many people buy cars to impress people but many times these cars attract the wrong attention and bring the wrong type of people into your life.

Don't Get Married, Unless...

I tell ALL men to never get married. There is just too much to lose and the system is rigged against you. It's like me encouraging men to take all their net worth to Vegas and gamble it while knowing that the house is against you. You have very little chance of winning that type of bet, so why bother. It's the same with marriage. Odds are, you're going to lose.

UNLESS you can outright divorce your wife and move on to another situation and you don't get financially fucked over. There is an outside chance that it could be possible, but for the majority of men, that is not the case. Donald Trump has seemed to make that work for him, but he also has a team of lawyers working for him that are looking out for his best interest. 99% of the men are not in that boat. If you're in that boat, go ahead and get married. The marriage laws are irrelevant to you.

If you're not that person though, don't get married! I don't care who you are, I don't care how hot the woman is, and I don't care if you don't ever think she will "do that to you." Do not get married! You cannot afford it.

Just like when you buy a car that you really can't afford and the car breaks down. You take it to the dealership and they tell you that the repair costs $3000 and you think, "Damn, I can't afford that..." Well then you can't afford the car! That's the same with marriage. When it breaks down, you can't afford to maintain it or correct it, so you shouldn't get into it in the first place.

This is the easiest way to avoid financial problems in the future.

Don't Finance Small Items

Financing small items like cell phones, toasters and small appliances is not worth it. People are actually financing smart phones for 2-3 year terms like it is a necessity. Smart phones are NOT a necessity. Does having one make your life easier at times, sure it does. Does having one bring you money or does it bleed money from your bank account? Does having one take your focus away from the priorities that you have in your life or does it add? Do you NEED the latest version of the smart phone or can you function with a version that is slightly outdated?

Why do you NEED the latest phone? Most of these phones come with new technology that is useless to you, but you think it makes a difference, so you overpay for them. Talking emojis and an improved camera is not enough to convince me to finance a phone that I could not afford to pay cash for. Overpay, I should say.

You can get a pre-paid phone at Target for cheaper that has technology that is on par with the latest updated smart phone. Nobody cares what type of phone you have, unless it's a better phone than they have. That only brings jealousy and envy into your space. You didn't get a pat on your back for it so WTF?

I've seen people that live in million dollars homes and have good salaries still carrying around phones that are four versions behind. I've also seen people who couldn't produce $1000 liquid cash out of their ass holding the latest smart phone and a bus pass.

Don't finance small items, don't finance microwaves and small appliances, clothes or things that they say will help you improve your credit. If you are using your credit card for these purchases and not immediately paying off the balance, you are paying far too much for these small items. Sometimes, you are paying double or triple the retail price in the end.

Use a Budget Spreadsheet to Track Your Spending

I use Excel or Numbers to create a monthly spreadsheet and I track how much I'm spending for everything. It breaks down all of my utilities, recurring payments, and monthly expenses. It also breaks down all my minor or miscellaneous expenses that I may incur such as dining out, grooming and birthday gifts. Once I've reached my budget for the month, I know that I must use my self-control on spending for whatever remains of that month or when new money comes in.

By intentionally tracking my money, I discover where I could save a little extra. $200 here and there can help change the direction of my finances and my life quite considerably.

Within my budget, I have a section called Murphy's Law, which is a cushion that basically is an additional emergency funding. It's the idea that "whatever will go wrong, will go wrong." Some things in life are out of our control and we can do nothing about them. But, we can have a few dollars prepared in our budget in case it does go wrong.

In my spread sheet, Murphy's Law could be 5-10% of your normal spending and if nothing goes wrong, you'll have extra dollars to work with and more cushion for the next month, which means more money saved.

Learn To Invest In the Market

This is how I learned to invest. I took $300 and I opened up an investment account online. There are many to choose from that have special offers to encourage you to open with them. Find the one that best fits what your needs are. I was cautious on how it worked so this small amount was a way for me to test it.

I purchase just a few shares in some major companies that I recognized and then I purchased multiple shares in small companies, called penny stocks (any stock that is valued between $2-15 per share). Then, I held on to them and tracked them to see if they grew or lost value. Most of them went up and down, while other stayed steady or increased. For those that increased, it was interesting to watch and learn how you can increase your money by doing little to nothing.

Using tools available online, you can get information about certain stocks to watch and companies that may have some news that could impact the stock's value. Yahoo Finance has a ranking of stocks in specific categories of companies (tech, energy, cannabis). They featured and ranked 25 companies in each category and track them. I would then purchase stock from a company on the list based on what I could afford and let the money ride. Since I was investing very little, it didn't have a great impact on my liquid financial status.

I would advise you to do this only if you do not need this money in the next 90 days. This is money that should not be touched. Periodically, I would make adjustments, but for the most part, I left it as is, since I don't have the time to manage it 24/7. To my amazement, many times, the money grew in small increments and like I said, I was doing very little to make this happen. Of course, the market is very sensitive, so there were loses as well. Learning about how the market works could mitigate your losses.

Crypto currency is another option for those looking to invest. It has a great learning curve and has already seen its peak action around 2017-2018. However silently now, people are still investing and seeing its potential to be a major player in the investment world, as there is a need for it in the future.

Once you have a substantial amount of money, you can hire a financial adviser to oversee your money. Just work closely with them and check your money every day! I had two clients that were financial advisers and each of them had their own requirements regarding how much money you would need to begin working with them. In some cases you may need $250,000-$500,000 to start with an adviser.

Fix Your Credit

Having good credit is how you are judged in relation to your financial responsibility, and ability to pay back creditors. I think everyone should have a good understanding on how credit works and how it positively or negatively affects your ability to secure financing and borrow money.

I'm not going to spend a lot of time discussing credit but do your research on maintaining your credit. Even though your goal is to purchase things with cash, having good credit when you need it will help you in the long run.

Check your credit at least twice a year. There was a time when I was scared to check my credit because I knew that I was a disaster. I didn't respect it until I needed it to rent apartments, apply for loans, or do background checks for my jobs. But once I started checking it, I discovered that there were things on there that didn't belong, such as non-collectable debt, items that I didn't purchase and items that I could dispute. For non-collectable debt, something can be on your credit report that based on your state law (statute of limitations), a creditor doesn't have the ability to collect the debt, but you still may be getting calls from those creditors. Sneaky like b*tches!

Having limited knowledge on your credit may actually restart the clock on your statute of limitations for non-collectable debt, which will negatively affect your credit. Do your research! These are the very things that I'm talking about spending your time on instead of chasing ass. Too many people showing me how much ass they're getting but their credit score looks like shit. They don't know the difference between a stock and a mutual fund and they can't tell me the current interest rate on their credit cards, but they are bragging about getting ass. Really?

You are entitled to a free credit report each year, but you can use services like Credit Karma to get updated news on your credit report and even put restriction on your credit to prevent identity theft. You can also get an idea on how your credit score fluctuates. Taking stock in your credit will allow you to get yourself in a healthier financial position and be a high level Free Agent.

Pay Cash for Everything

If you haven't learned anything from me, please let this be what you remember: Pay Cash for Everything! EVER-Y-THING. If you cannot pay cash for something that you want, then you don't need it. If you do not have five times what the item costs in your bank account or under your mattress, you do not need to buy it. If you're using credit for small items, groceries and cameras, do not purchase it. You are not ready to buy it. You're going to end up paying 3-4 times more for these items since your only paying the minimum payment of your credit card each month. If you cannot buy it outright with cash, you can't afford. This is a simple principle that doesn't need much more explaining.

Don't Buy Too Much House or Rent Too Much Apartment

Since the McMansion explosion of early 2000's, many of us find that we are committing ourselves to too much space when there is no need. Many times when we do that, we are just trying to impress others with our homes.

There are many people living in 3000-5000 square foot homes when their parents grew up in less than 1600 sq. feet. When there are only one or two people living in a space, why do you need 3000 sq. feet of space?

One person can live in a studio apartment (about 500 square feet) if needed. Having more space, just to have it or impress other people who don't even like you, is a waste of resources and a waste of time. You have to maintain that house and eventually the house will start to run your life and those costs will be eating up your finances.

Many people got into trouble during the great housing bubble by buying way too much house than they could afford. Some people lost their homes; some people still live in these homes today because they are underwater on the loan. This is what happens when you view something that is clearly a liability as an asset or investment. Study Robert Kiyosaki's book Rich Dad, Poor Dad, or Cash Flow Quadrant to get a better understanding of this. This mistake is bound to happen in future generations, which is a shame because we know so much already.

The explosion of the minimalist philosophy, tiny homes, full-time RV living is bringing back the idea of purchasing only what is necessary. The gentrification of neighborhoods that are closer to the city is also restoring the idea of buying only the space that you need.

If someone I meet is not happy with my space, then they don't need to be there. Don't allow people who are not investing in your home to dictate what type or size of home you should live in.

Often times, the space that we are buying is not even livable space. If you want to buy those types of homes, buy them as investment properties. Maybe you live in a large home and rent out the rooms and pay for your mortgage with the room rents that you're charging. Or maybe you don't want to live with roommates, so you rent a small apartment, live in a tiny home/RV or a smaller house for yourself and rent the larger home out to tenants.

It's funny, when I mention the idea of becoming a landlord; everyone wants to talk about how hard it is, or the nightmares about managing tenants and properties. So as an alternative, they turn their large homes into money pits, when they can actually use it to create passive income. Some people love avoiding work.

Living in a fancy apartment or large home to attract some ass actually results in costing you more money. These types of women will look at your living situation and your fancy financed vehicle and think you have money to burn, but in reality you're in debt up to your eyeballs. Besides that, you have way more maintenance and utility costs than one person needs.

I'm not telling you to not buy a home, although I can share my philosophy about real estate as an investment at another time. But, buying a four plex may be better financially as opposed to buying a large home to live in it all by yourself. You're losing money when your property could actually be generating more money.

For My Married Brothers – Take Back Control of Your Checking Account

If you are a married man and you see the writing on the wall regarding the status of said marriage, the best thing you can do is take back control of your checking account.

If you have a shared bank account where you funds are being co-mingled and you have given your wife access or control over that account, you are screwed if/when things fall apart. You're an idiot if you still have this type of arrangement. You're living in the 1950's marital fantasy lore. And, she has somehow duped you into doing so. Why? Because she can spend your money, while the money that she produces can be spent on her. What's his is hers and what's hers is hers.

Do not turn your finances over to your wife! She may tell you that she knows how to manage money, but women don't manage money, they spend money. Men manage money.

For instance, when bills roll in, women will pay the bills as they come in the door, despite having a tight budget. Paying bills like this could leave you in a lurch should you run out of money. You may end up with not enough money to put gas in your tank until the next direct deposit hits. You pay your bills on time, but make sure you manage the flow of how they are paid. That is managing money. Just spending the money that is in the account is NOT managing money.

Get control of YOUR accounts back from your wife and watch over them yourself. When that divorce rape starts coming towards your front door, you can then move money where you need to fend off the assault she is about to unleash on your monkey ass.

CHAPTER

10

PEACE, QUIET AND FREEDOM

If you made it this far, you're ready to become an unrestricted Free Agent.

When you focus on the things that matter, the P-Sleeve should no longer have control on you. Not saying that you will not want it or be attracted to it, but you start to have the understanding that the best thing for you is to start thinking with your big head, instead of with your little head.

We are fortunate to be in this life. It's a miracle that we won the genetic race to our mother's egg. But, this is not a dress rehearsal or a practice for the life that we want to live the next time we're here. This is it! This is the one life that we get to receive everything out of it that we possibly can.

We are past the point of being providers for individuals who don't appreciate us, other than using us to obtain the things that they can't get on their own. They don't respect us or appreciate us, and it shows. Just turn on the news and see how much women are complaining about the things they are not receiving and at the same time not willing to give anything up in return. Ultimately, they will use the system to extract those same resources from you should you choose to not fall in line with their agenda.

So, the mythical love is not our pursuit. Peace, Quiet and Freedom (PQF) is what we are looking for. When we choose PQF, everything about our lives improve exponentially. We begin to focus on the things that matter rather than trying to convince people that we should matter to them.

Start reading and focus on bettering yourself for the life that you can provide for yourself. Not bettering or improving yourself for women or others. We are beyond that point.

We're not bettering ourselves for women to date. We're not bettering ourselves for society. We're not bettering ourselves to become better mates and providers for others. We're putting our best foot forward for ourselves!

There is real power in your commitment. If you give your commitment away too easily without showing value, they will never respect you. At that point, you're nothing to them; they can get rid of you. You are disposable! It's one of the reasons why you shouldn't commit to anyone unless you have demonstrated high value and then you can be more selective and have more options to pick from. That person will be more appreciative of your efforts and respect you. You want these individuals to give you their best effort at all times. In today's social climate, this is near impossible. People are too fickle, and getting involved emotionally carries too much risk. So, *PEACE, QUIET & FREEDOM* is the best possible choice

Prioritize Your Fun

I want you to have fun in this life. I want you to have fun in life from your teenage years until the age of 80. I want you to imagine yourself still doing the things that you enjoyed to do when you were 18, because you still can.

Society wants you to believe that you're going to grow old and be useless. Marriage encourages us to settle down and sit on a porch swing with some old lady and just wait for death to creep around the corner.

You can go to certain regions in the United States and witness ageless people living their best life, doing active things, things that bring them a lot of pleasure, and they are not the image of the mid-western grand pappy at age 55. I don't want that to be you. I still want you to be an active participant in your life.

You need to maximize your time in the best way that it can work for you. A lot of times, we put too much time and resources into trying to appeal to women. This book is not telling you to not have contact with women. What I want you to understand is that if you prioritize women in your life, not only will you end up with the short end of the stick; you will end up with less resources and energy because you are putting those resources towards her. You will end up not having much fun because you are using your time trying to entertain and please her, and women are not to be pleased. It is not your duty to provide entertainment for her and be a dancing monkey to keep her happy. You are fighting a losing battle if you choose to take that role in her life.

If you make a long term commitment to her, you're going to lose a lot of your resources, so prioritizing yourself and prioritizing your fun will give you the best quality life bar none.

When you decide to live this way, people will call you selfish. But ask yourself, "What are you here for?" Am I supposed to be here to give everything that I earn to someone else? When you hear statements like that, it is just to guilt-trip you into conforming back into society's expectations of the provider male.

Some men get guilted out of enjoying the things that they love, by men and women alike. If you have toys, play with toys. If you ride motorcycles, ride the hell out of them. This is YOUR life! Do what you want to do.

You're here to enjoy your best life. You're here to enjoy a good quality life. You're not here to be a provider of resources and entertainment for everyone else.

Because of the work that I do, I have a limited amount of time to pursue the things that I enjoy. When women ask to spend time with me, it will be doing something that I enjoy doing, not something that they want to do. I enjoy my long list of hobbies and they bring me much more enjoyment than any woman could ever offer. Too often, women use men as emotional tampons, transferring the energy and drama of their lives onto us. Women call this "listening to her," but in reality this is just killing us softly. All you're thinking is "I wish she would shut the fuck up so I can play Call of Duty."

Your things come first. Nobody else's stuff comes before you. You do your recess first. You do your recreation first. This is for your mental sanity. The more time that you spend with women, the higher the likelihood that things will go off the rails. It's the law of diminishing returns. How many times have you spent 4-6 hours with a woman, only to have the evening end with an argument or disagreement that kills the entire vibe? You cannot make her happy, but you can surely make yourself happy in numerous ways.

Women are not very entertaining. They are actually pretty boring. If you take the "sex factor" out, women don't provide much entertainment or value. Mainly because they expect you to entertain them.

I remember having weeks where I would have four to five different women in my bed and still feel empty. Sex felt like I was just shaking another hand, there was no connection, and I wished I had spent my time doing something else.

Take six months from dating and save $50-60 a week that you

would've blown on a date with a woman and use it on the things that bring you much more happiness than you would get by prioritizing women. So enjoy the things that you can.

The 90-Day Commitment

If you want to conquer the world, start off by making your bed. Every single day! This is something that I have done since college. I can't leave my house without my bed made, because if I return to an unmade bed, I might just want to jump back in it. A made bed discourages laziness on many levels. And, don't think you're about to conquer anything with an unmade bed waiting for you at home.

When you want to make a major change in your life, you have to make a commitment to yourself to do just that. And, I think 90 days is the right amount of time to give yourself to commit to a life changing process. No longer will you accept the excuses that you tell yourself. These things have got to get done. I don't care what you have going on in your life, the things that you have on your daily list have to get done without fail. No interference; No excuses.

Making something become a habit takes time. For instance kicking the fast food bug doesn't happen overnight. You have to slowly pull away from it and over time you'll actually be disgusted to set foot inside one of those "restaurants."

If you can continue to do something over a 90-day period, then it will become a part of who you are. It will not require as much effort as it does when you initially start.

Here are some simple changes that you can make in your life that will shift the direction of your life:

- Diet / Meal Planning

- Saving Money
- Exercise Programs
- Doing More Hobbies
- Getting Out Of A Toxic Relationship
- Giving Up Dating/Dating Apps
- Waking Up Early

When you begin doing these things, it will initially make you uncomfortable. In order to make a necessary change in your life, you must fully commit to the process, no matter what the results are along the way.

So, I encourage you brothers to set up a 90-day challenge for an area that you want to see change in your life. Start the process and do not check the results until the 90 days are over. If you check the results too soon after starting the program, you might get discouraged at the progress or lack of progress that you've made. This leads to abandoning your program well before it's time to get an accurate picture of the results.

Success That I've Had During 90 Day Commitments

Giving Up Dating Apps

Nothing will free up your time like this. Witness the amount of clarity and free thought that you are able to process without returning regurgitated messages to an endless wasteland of potential one night stands that you will nominate to limit your potential in life. Once I gave up dating apps, my entire life improved and I stopped banging 6's who thought they were entitled to be treated like 9's.

Starting My Social Media Platforms

Before I began making social media content on YouTube and Instagram, I was sitting in my bedroom with thoughts in my head about starting social media. I knew I had a lot to say, but I didn't know how to get started. Finally, I literally said "f*ck it," and started posting hardcore for 90 days. I started off my YouTube channel with 500 subscribers and six months later I had over 40,000. This changed my life because it allowed me to offer help to men in a way that is not available to them.

Workout Programs

I worked as a private fitness trainer and many clients wanted to check their progress each training session. But, many of those clients hadn't worked out for over two years and they believed that working out once or twice would yield them immediate results. Well, if it worked that way, then all anyone would have to do is get fat over 3-4 years, then work it all off in 2-3 months. What possible change could occur in the time? Not much.

However, if you look at the results from when you started and the results from when you ended the 90-day commitment, you will see a significant change, and the path that you've created will start you on a brand new path. It will actually change your life. It will move you into a position that you didn't think was possible.

I know that we live in a microwave society where people want things now, and refuse to wait longer than it takes a pop tart to warm up, but that's not how life works. There is no magic pill to this life. You must put in the work to get the results.

I spoke on many areas that men should be focusing on that many of us let fall apart. Many times, men have the time to manage these areas but would rather spend excessive amount of time pursuing women, and when they fail with women, they spend time and resources trying to figure out where they failed. But, their beds remain unmade, their job statuses are shaky, their credits are shitty, and they can't produce four figures of money within 24 hours. It's time to focus on your life and to prioritize it. The Free Agent Lifestyle is your next step to getting everything you can out of this life.

FREE AGENT STATUS: VERIFIED

Congratulations! You are now ready to be a FREE AGENT!

You have been equipped to deal with a multitude of scenarios regarding life, women, and choices. You are released from the restrictions that may have been limiting you, and commitments that have been holding you back. You've seen the proverbial light at the end of the tunnel and ahead is enlightenment, PEACE, QUIET, and FREEDOM.

If you feel that this message helped you in any way, feel free to share this book title with someone. Many men prefer to deal with some of their issues in private, and sharing this may give them some options that they haven't considered. Maybe they have sought out professional counseling and it didn't work or maybe they hit a rough patch in their life and need a boost.

Either way, I appreciate you taking the time to read these words. Go live your best life, the life that you were entitled to.

PEACE!

COACH GREG ADAMS

ABOUT THE AUTHOR

Coach Greg Adams is a life/divorce coach and motivational speaker. He has worked in the fitness industry as an independent fitness trainer since 2013 and has helped hundreds of men and women change their lives by reaching their fitness goals. He worked previously a college basketball coach for over 15 years. He is featured on the Coach Greg Adams YouTube Channel and can be heard on the Free Agent Lifestyle podcast. For more information, please visit social media platforms, www.gregadamsone.com or www.thefreeagentlifestyle.com

Printed in Great Britain
by Amazon

75859527R00068